HOW TO BECOME A *Lingerie* DESIGNER
BY LAURIE VAN JONSSON

www.howtobecomealingeriedesigner.com

Have you ever thought of wanting to make your own lingerie? Then this book is for you. Want to understand about patterns, costing or grading? Or maybe you are studying fashion and need some assistance? Whatever your reason; you can find the answers on the following pages. This book will touch upon everything you need to help you start, or market your lingerie.

This book is designed to give you the answers you need and save you months of trawling the Internet for information. At the end of the book are interviews from current lingerie designers, who gave very honest answers to the questions I asked them. Just like you, all they started out with was vision and determination.

How to become a Lingerie Designer

HOW TO BECOME A *Lingerie* DESIGNER

BY LAURIE VAN JONSSON

Book Contents

Introduction

LINGERIE

Chapter One

Lingerie
A BRIEF HISTORY

Pre 1900s
1900-1910s
1910s
1920s
1930s
1940s
1950s
1960s
1970s – 1980s
1980s onwards to date
The future

Chapter Two

Inspiration
FOR DESIGNING

Where do i get inspiration from?
Copyright Laws
Useful onloine resources
Print & Online
Fabrics

Chapter Three

Target
MARKET

What is market analysis?
Identifying your target market
Trouble identifying your target market
The direction of your brand
Keeping on track

Chapter Four   *Sketchbooks*
                                 & MOOD BOARDS

The importance of a sketch book
Style of mood boards
Designing mood boards

Chapter Five   *Fashion*
                                 DRAWINGS

Fashion drawing styles
Help with fashion drawing
Fashion drawing
How to convert a drawing to a finished piece

Chapter Six   *Working*
                                 DRAWINGS

The importance of working drawings
Basic working drawings

Chapter Seven   *Patterns*

Pattern books
The History of patterns
How to create a pattern
Using the same pattern
Making a brief block pattern
Front brief
Information on a pattern
Gusset pattern
Back brief
Back brief pattern

Chapter Eight   *Bra*
                                 PATTERNS

Soft Bra
Pattern pieces of a Bra
The Bra Wire
Components of a Bra

Chapter Nine

Specification
SHEETS

What is a specification sheet?
Why use spec sheets?
What goes on a spec sheet?
Measuring a 'brief' for a spec sheet
Measurementsof a brief
Using Excel for your spec sheet
Measuring a 'soft bra' for a spec sheet
Key measurements for an underwired bra
Measurements for a 'soft bra'.
Underwire bra measurements

Chapter Ten

Grading

What is grading?
Grading the front brief
Understanding bra grading
Cross grading a bra
Grading a bra
When not to use a standard grade

Chapter Eleven

Sample
SPEC SHEETS

What are sample spec sheets?
What to put on the sample sheet

Chapter Twelve

Costings

How important is understanding costings?
Costing with bigger companies
Measuring elastics to cost
Measuring fabric to cost
Example cost sheet
Blank costing sheet: Free permission to use
Mark up

Chapter Thirteen **Manufacturing**
The decline of UK lingerie manufacturing.
Global manufacturing
Hand made Vs Factory manufacturing
Current UK Manufacturers

Chapter Fourteen **Photoshoots**
Studio Vs Location
Video of the photoshoot

Chapter Fifteen **Additional**
ITEMS TO CONSIDER
Website, Business Cards, Product labelling

Chapter Sixteen **Networking**
Contacting lingerie buyers
The importance of newsletters
The Pros and the Cons of 'Sale or Return'
Exhibiting at a trade show
List of trade shows

Chapter Seventeen **Press Releases**
Creating a press release
Formatting a press release.
Sample of old press releases (circa 2005)
Working with Journalists

Chapter Eighteen **Lingerie**
COURSES
Expanding your knowledge base.

Final Words
Interviews with Lingerie Designers
Book Reviews
Handy Websites
References

How to become a Lingerie Designer

HOW TO BECOME A *Lingerie* DESIGNER

Have you ever wanted to make your own lingerie? Then this book is for you. Want to understand patterns? Learn about costings or grading? Maybe you are studying fashion and need some assistance?

This book will give you an insight on how to make or market your lingerie. Touching on patterns and cost sheets, fabrics and working drawings, list of trade shows, templates of specification sheets, and tips on how to develop your designs. Also included is advice about the technical side of designing lingerie and where to go for further information. This book has been designed to cover all aspects of designing lingerie and attempts to incorporate all topics but you may want to know further in depth information which is touched upon.

What's not in this book is how to write a business plan. It only covers what I have directly learnt from the lingerie industry. There are plenty of books or courses written about this by people who have more knowledge about implementing and devising these plans.

So am I qualified to write this book? In short Yes.

The longer version: I have over 14 years in the lingerie industry. I graduated in the year 2000 with a BA (HONS) Fashion & Textiles taking the Contour path. From there I worked in a design team for a UK manufacturer, designing lingerie and swimwear for UK high street stores under their own label. Stores such as Top Shop, Next, River Island, Etam and Tammy Girl.

I have worked abroad in Thailand designing swimwear. Free-lanced for numerous companies, in women's and men's fashion including under and outerwear. Launched my own lingerie label 'Vanjo'. Given presentations and lectured fashion classes at University. Worked in Australia designing for the high streets, and as this book goes to print; I am currently in the process of gaining my Masters in Fashion design. On top of this I have gathered extra qualifications in Computer Grading, Fashion Styling, Fashion Journalism, Copy Writing and Business Management.

My most relevant work to this book is the Lingerie label I ran: Vanjo. Designing Lingerie for sizes C cup to FF cup and going down to a 28-inch back. I used fabrics that were rarely found in the bigger cup market, and applied them to get the best fit. Additionally I understood how distinct fabrics gave differing support and began altering my patterns each time accordingly. It was whilst running my label that I noticed other designers launching their own "Lingerie Labels" who had no previous experience in the lingerie trade. Designers who became really successful; starting their own label, with just a concept and a dream. Many even started off without the ability to grade with no previous technical knowledge. Spending painstaking months trying to learn it all themselves as they went along.

Are you ready to be that successful Lingerie Designer?

For those who have had a glimpse into the fashion world will know, that sometimes you have to be ruthless to succeed. Companies do not want to divulge where they sourced their fabrics or trims. Who they use as their manufacturer or which trade shows to attend. Why doesn't anyone share this information?

Well mainly because it's taken them months maybe years, to source that very thing that is making them successful. This led me to believe how great it would be to be able to get all the information in one place. One book. This book...

The fact is there are many wonderful and talented designers out there, who haven't had any training, who are spending months maybe years trying to start out. Is that you?

This book is not a short cut to rid you of working hard to achieve your dream, but it will cut down those months of trying to figure everything out by yourself. It covers the basics to get you started so you can be a complete novice or build on the information you already possess. It'll give you a starting point. A glimpse into the lingerie industry; it will help guide you and enable you to understand the basics of being a lingerie designer. Although different companies differ on how they do their specification or sample sheets, fundamentally the information is the same.

This book is designed to give you the answers you need and save you months of trawling the Internet for information. At the end of this book are interviews from current lingerie designers, who gave very honest answers to the questions I asked them. Just like you they started out with just a vision and determination.

I wish you all the very best success.
Laurie van Jonsson x

"...Success is the sum of small efforts, repeated day in and day out..."

Robert Collier

Chapter One

Lingerie
A BRIEF HISTORY

The actual term 'lingerie' was not in widespread use until the late 1850's. The word originates from the Old French word linge meaning "linen". The term 'lingerie' was originally introduced into the English language as a euphemism for scandalous underclothing. Lingerie throughout the years has helped define beauty; while at the same time revealing a great deal about a society's cultural and political values. From false buttocks and wasp waists, to the uplifted breasts of the 1990s. The lingerie market of the 21st century is far different today from how it began. With modern fabrics and technological advancements such as laser-cut seamless bras, molded T-shirt bras and foundation wear; a woman nowadays can design her own silhouette. With more choice than ever you can stay with basics, treat yourself to silks, or simply indulge your fantasies and design yourself the most lavish lingerie you can imagine.

Pre 1900s

According to Life magazine, Herminie Cadolle (of France) invented the first modern bra in 1889. It appeared in a corset catalogue as a two-piece undergarment. This garment basically cut the traditional corset in two, the lower part was a corset for the waist, the upper supporting the breasts by means of shoulder straps. The description reads "designed to sustain the bossom and supported by the shoulders". She patented her invention and showed at the Great Exhibition of 1889. In 1893 Marie Tucek received a U.S. patent for a device, that consisted of separate pockets for each breast above a metal supporting plate and shoulder straps fastened by hook-and-eye. This invention more closely resembled the modern bra known today and was a precursor to the underwire bra. Though it was marketed unsuccessfully.
By 1905 the upper half was being sold separately as a soutien-gorge, the name by which bras are still known in France.

1900-1910s

Throughout history people have used a variety of garments and devices to cover, restrain, or elevate their breasts. In the 1900s garments were portrayed with shoulder supports, with little adaptability. At this stage the major appeal was for those, whose lung function and mobility was a priority rather than what it looked like.
Bras became widely promoted over the course of the 1910s. As women began participating in more sports and vigorous dancing, they began to throw out their corsets in favor of more comfortable brassieres.

1910s

On November 3, 1914, the U.S. Patent Office issued a patent to Mary P. Jacob for the Backless Brassiere.

Although it was not the first bra to be commercially produced in the U.S., Jacob's patent was the first to be registered in the newly created patent category for "brassieres". This has led Jacob's invention, generally to receive credit as the first U.S. bra patent. (U.S. bra patents appear as far back as the 1860s, but were generally filed in the "corsets" category).

This invention came about in 1910 when Mary P Jacob (known also as Polly) was preparing to go to a debutante ball. Polly who was generously endowed had worn this dress previously and didn't like the whale bones from her corset poking up out the front.

She worked with her maid Marie to put together two silk handkerchiefs with pink ribbon and cord. The design went from strength to strength and when a stranger approached her to sell the brassiere she knew it could become a viable business. Although her design flattened rather than flattered; which was in keeping with the 1920s flapper style; her business never really took off. After a few years she sold the patent to Warners. Warner went on to earn more than fifteen million dollars from the bra patent over the next thirty years.

The bra became popular during the First World War; this was in part due to the gender role changing. This era saw many women work in factories and wear uniforms for the first time. Additionally the social attitudes towards women at this time helped to liberate them from corsets.

This co-insided with the U.S. War Industries Board who in 1917 asked women to stop buying corsets to free up metal for war production. This apparently saved around 28,000 tons of metal enough to build two battleships.

1920s

By 1920 although providing less support than the corset the bust was now contained in a brassiere. The brassiere was a shaped Bandeau that clipped on to the corset, holding everything in and down. A low sloping bustline became more fashionable. This gave a more boyish figure which was inkeeping with, the "Flapper Era". This style downplayed women's curves; it was easy for small-busted women to follow the flat chested look. Women with larger breasts had to try garments; like the "Symington Side Lacer" which laced both sides, to flatten the chest.

In 1922 Russian immigrant Ida Rosenthal was a seamstress at the dress shop Enid Frocks in New York City. Ida and her husband William Rosenthal, along with shop owner Enid Bissett changed the look of women's fashion forever. They founded a company called 'Maidenform manufacturing company'. The company was established because they noticed that when a bra fitted one woman, it did not fit another woman who was the same dress size. From this they went about and developed the concept of cup size. Their innovation was designed to make the dresses they made, look better on the wearer. They increased the shaping of the bandeau bra to enhance and support women's breasts: hence the name "Maidenform". Maidenform accented and uplifted the bust rather than flattening it, and so the modern 'supportive' uplifting bra was born.

The major changes in design were the appearance of distinct cups, backless bras, underwiring and newer fabrics. These fashion changes coincided with health professionals campaigning against breast flattening. Research had suggested a link with breast care and comfort to both mother and infant during lactation. The emphasis shifted from minimizing the breasts to uplifting and accenting them. Women and especially the younger set welcomed the bra as a modern garment. In 1927 nursing bras were introduced when William Rosenthal, the president of Maidenform took out brassiere design patents including nursing, full figured and the first seamed uplift bra.

1930s

In 1935, Warners developed what they called the 'Alphabet Bra', the bra consisted of four sizes A, B, C & D (Double-D came later and Double-A later still). In the UK, this standard was not adopted until the 1950s. They used Junior and Medium sizing until this point.

Women started taking a greater interest in the size of their breasts, as a result bras rapidly became a major industry during the 1930s. Improvements in technology, fabrics, colours, and patterns led to bras succeeding finanically far better than the retail industry overall. Innovations included Warners' use of elastic, the adjustable strap, the sized cup, and padded bras for smaller-breasted women. Department stores developed fitting areas and manufacturers even arranged fitting training courses for saleswomen. Other major manufacturers of the 30s included Triumph, Maidenform, Gossard, Courtaulds, Spirella, Spencer, Twilfit, and Symington. The desired silhouette of the 1930s was a pointy bust which further increased demand for a forming garment.

The word 'brassiere' became shortened to 'bra' in the 1930s, initially by young college women and in 1939 the word bra was added to the English dictionary.

1940s

The Second World War had a major impact on the clothing industry. The materials that were used to make undergarments such as steel and rubber were in short supply so manufactures turned to synthetic materials; this eventually lead to Lycra, Rayon, and Latex.

Military women of lower rank were fitted with uniform underwear. Dress codes appeared, for example Lockheed informed their workers that bras must be worn because of 'good taste, anatomical support, and morale'. Military terminology, such as the pointed Torpedo or Bullet bra started to appear in the 1940-50s, designed for 'maximum projection'.

A new image was the Sweater Girl, - a busty and wholesome 'girl next door' whose tight fitting outer garments accentuated her artificially enhanced curves. Sweater Girls often wore bullet bras. The image portrayed by actresses like Jane Russell; who wore the "lift and separate" design went on to influence the development of later brassieres.

Following the Second World War, material availability, production and demand slowly recovered. A postwar baby boom created huge demand for maternity and nursing bras.

Meanwhile in America, during the 1940s the push-up bra was being invented by Frederick Mellinger who had started his own lingerie business. A year later he moved to Hollywood and the retail lingerie store, Frederick's of Hollywood was born. This was the first time lingerie was created for style instead of practicality, and Frederick's pieces were famous among many Hollywood stars.

1950s

The glamour of the 1950s once again valued the hourglass figure, and lingerie manufactures began to flourish and were soon launching their own brand names to build customer loyalty.
A recovering postwar economy fueled demands for consumer goods with greater variety. Manufacturers met this with new fabrics, colours, patterns, and styles. Padding and stretch ability were among other innovations. Hollywood glamour became an increasingly powerful influence in fashion.

1960s

During the 1960s bra designers and manufacturers began introducing padded bras and bras with underwire. There was an increase in the interest in quality and fashion. Maternity and mastectomy bras began to gain a new respectability, and the increasing use of washing machines created a need for products that were more durable. The bra continued to evolve.

In the late 1960s, some of the emblems of femininity became targets of feminist activism. Feminists stated that bras reduced women to the status of sex objects. Some women publicly disavowed their bras in an anti-sexist act of female liberation. When Germaine Greer stated that, "Bras are a ludicrous invention", her statement resonated with many women who had been questioning the role of the bra.
In September 1968 a 'Freedom Trash Can' was placed on the ground, and filled with bras, high-heeled shoes, false eyelashes, girdles, curlers, hairspray, makeup, corsets, magazines (such as Playboy), and other items thought to be "instruments of torture". Someone suggested lighting a fire, but a permit could not be obtained, and so (contrary to the subsequent urban legend) there was no bra burning, nor did anyone take off their bra.

1970s - 1980s

The perception of undergarments changed, and in the 1970s more comfortable and natural looking bras grew in popularity. In response to the feminist era, many bra manufacturers' marketing claimed that wearing their bra was like "not wearing a bra".

The evolution of the bra reflected the constant changing idea of what the 'ideal' woman should look like—flat, round, pointy, conical, or even natural. The contemporary bra also reflects advances in manufacturing and availability of fabric types and colours. Enabling the bra to be transformed from a utilitarian item to a fashion statement, countering the negative attitudes some women held about bras. Designers also incorporated numerous devices to produce varying shapes, cleavage, and to give women bras they could wear with open-back dresses, off-the-shoulder dresses, and plunging necklines.

1980s Onwards to date

Since the mid-1990s, women have more choice in bra sizes. A variety of styles now come in sizes from 26-52 inch backs, from an AAA to K in cup sizes. Lingerie has started to fall into two categories: undergarments designed with function and modesty in mind, and lingerie that is racier mainly worn in the bedroom and designed for show.

By the 1990s, Fredericks of Hollywood and Victoria Secrets became two of America's largest lingerie retail chains. The design of lingerie started to become fashionable rather than solely functional.

By 2003 the global lingerie market was estimated at $29 Billion American dollars. In the European market it is fragmented, with Triumph International and DB Apparel leading the market.
There is now a wide range of brassiere styles available designed to match different body types, situations, and outer garments.
The degree of shaping and coverage of the breasts varies between styles, as well as the function. Common types include backless, balconette, convertible, cupless, demi cup, front-fastening, full coverage, halter, longline, minimizing, padded, plunge, push-up, racerback, sports/athletic, sheer, strapless, strapless-backless, t-shirt, underwire, wireless, sports bra, and invisible.

*More information about different styles of bras can be found in the book "The Anatomy of the Bra".

The Future

Two design challenges that bra manufacturers face at present seem conflicting. On one hand there is a demand for minimal bras that allow plunging necklines and reduce interference with the lines of outer garments, such as the shelf bra. On the other hand, body mass and bust size is increasing leading to a higher demand for larger sizes. Over a 10 year period, the most common size purchased in the UK went from 34B to 36C.

In 2001, 27 percent of UK sales were for a D cup or larger. In addition there is slow recognition that the way women are being measured is no longer correct. When bras first appeared they were made from non stretch fabric, therefore when a women's ribcage was measured +4/5inches was added onto the figure, to allow ease of wear for the garment.

The common bra size is now changing, due to the stretch ability of the bra, women are now being fitted to their actual rib size. It's now not uncommon for a women who has been wearing a 36C, suddenly finding herself comfortably in 30E; having done nothing more than merely gone to a modern day fitter.

The brassiere is worn by the majority of women in Western society, even with an unprecedented array of styles to choose from, some women, health professionals, feminists and fashion writers appear to be increasingly questioning its place and function, and ask whether the bra will disappear, like the pantyhose, garter belt and stocking did. Bras though account for a billion-dollar industry that continues to grow, so currently it looks like bras are here to stay.

* For those, who wish to gain a more in depth knowledge of the 'History of the Brassiere' References can be found at the back of the book.

How to become a Lingerie Designer

Chapter Two

Inspiration
for DESIGNING

We all need a starting point, and it's from this point that inspiration occurs. This is the most exciting part of designing. A chance to draw on all the images and designs we see around us. Transforming them into something else, into your own designs.

Without inspiration you can't refine your ideas, you'll find yourself being pulled in different directions. But by gathering all the things that inspire you and putting them in your sketch book (see chapter four) you'll be able to see the direction you want to head in.

There is however, a fine line between inspiration and imitation, the latter of which should only be considered at your own peril. Imitation will typically lead you down a very narrow path due to what you are copying already having been successfully produced. Inspiration is taking an idea and developing it, imitation is taking an idea and using it as it already stands.

If you want to be a great designer, you want people to be able to see your designs and link them to your brand; not look at your designs and think that they are from another more established brand otherwise you will never set yourself apart and have your own style. Inspiration can come from anywhere, it could come from personal needs. You may want to design a concept, to inject into the market with something that isn't out there already. It could just come from things you find inspiring or beautiful; be that fabrics, trims, photographs, places of travel, magazine cuttings, music, the list goes on....

On the next few pages are a list of magazines and websites which can start to help you become inspired.

Before you go any further please bear in mind one of the most important pieces of advice; if you want to start your own brand - in order to succeed as a designer you have to develop your own signature style.

opyright Laws

Currently it's hard to get a copyright on your designs, and to be honest with the fast pace that fashion moves designers don't really bother. It can take 18 months for a patent to go through and by the time that happens the design will probably be out of fashion.

> 'Historically, fashion designers have been denied copyright protection because courts decided that ultilitarian articles should not be protected by copyright. The courts also decide not to give the copyright protection to designers who have complained about fast fashion knock-offs, because designers have not been able to demonstrate that it has hurt their business. '
> Quote taken from Observatory,   www.designobservatory.com

As this book goes to print, there is a bill that has been trying to be passed for the last few years in America, that allows for certain overall designs to have a copyright lasting three years. 'Chuck Schumer' who put forward this bill, seems unwilling to take no for an answer. Congress have already declined the bill six times. At the end of Jan 2013 the Bill of 'Innovative Design Protection Act' (IDPA) was again not enacted. This bill will have to be reintroduced if any change to the Copyright laws are to change in the future regarding this oversight.

At the minute, because of the speed at which high street stores can replicate and reproduce a design, designers are pushed to come up with new innovative designs and styles whilst keeping in with their own look. To replicate a garment for the high street stores, designers currently only have to make a few alterations for it to be acceptable. Some designers will even perform the 'squint test' against your design and a designer piece. If you can't tell the difference when squinting your eyes then you may still have to change your design slightly.

Even though there is no set copyright on designs, the lingerie designer 'Damaris' well known for her bum cleavage back bow knickers, sparked a craze of copiers including New look, River Island and the lingerie brand 'Myla', back in 2004. She did manage to settle out of court for the likeness of her design.

Useful Resources Online
A list of international websites or magazines for inspiration.

Worth Global Style Network - *www.wgsn.com*
WGSN is a leading online trend-analysis and research service, it provides information for the fashion and style industry. It was launched in 1998, is worldwide, and has over five million images and 650,000 pages of information. It also provides information on the following areas.

- *News*: Coverage of international and regional reports about the fashion industry.
- *Think Tanks*: A look at future trends in design.
- *Creative direction*: Information on product from across the industry, including key looks, emerging trends and inspiration.
- *Trade shows and catwalks*: pictures from catwalks and an inside view of trade shows.

PROMOSTYL - *www.promostyl.com*
Promostyl is an international trend research and design agency, which has been running for over forty years; it provides information on all the phases of your brand, product information and trend boards.

PRINT & ONLINE

Lingerie magazines or lingerie blogs are a great way to keep up to date with what is happening in the lingerie industry; whilst fashion magazines are the ideal opportunity to gain the real inspiration from. Taking ideas from outerwear and transposing the inspiration into lingerie. There are many magazines online and in print, far too many to suggest but here are a selective few.

LINGERIE MAGAZINES

Blint - *www.blint.es*
A leading trade magazine in Spain, Reports from international fairs and fashion catwalks, with detailed information regarding intimate apparel, swimwear and hosiery. There are 3 issues produced annually.

BodyGuide - *www.bodyguideonline.com*
An US intimate apparel industry guide. A sister publication to 'Body Magazine' which is produced twice a year.

Body Magazine - *www.bodymagazine.us*
An intimate apparel trade magazine for the US, covers all catergories of intimate apparel, and is published monthly.

Creations Lingerie - *www.creations-lingerie.com*
A French intimate apparel magazine, which gives reports and detailed news about the apparel industry. Four annual publications.

Intima - *www.intima.fr*
Launched in 1989, provides an indepth analysis on selected lingerie markets around the world. Four publications come out each year, once a year Intima published 'Intima Bain' a 200 page supplement which concentrates on beachwear.

Intimo piu mare - *www.intimopiumare.com*
A Italian magazine featuring intimates and swimwear, taken from top
Italian designer creations. Magazine includes information about trade
shows, fabric revews and technological development reports.

Lace n Lingerie - *www.lacenlingerie.com*
Founded in 1998, it was the first magazine to be published in India
about lingerie. Published bi-monthly.

Linea Intima - *www.lineaintima.net*
The first Italian Lingerie and Beachwear magazine started in 1957.
Six publications are published each year.

Linea Intima Asia - *www.intimasia.com*
An English written Lingerie magazine that started in 1996, providing
fashion trends as well as an insight into the Asian market and it's key
players. Two publications are out each year.

Lingerie Buyer - *www.lingerie-buyer.com*
A UK lingerie magazine launched in 1992, with latest news, views
and opinions, the magazine provides a complete overview of the
industry. Eight publications are available each year.

Lingerie Insight - *www.lingerieinsight.com*
The only monthly UK lingerie magazine, providing global lingerie
trends, business advice from retailers, wholesalers and designers and
facts and figures of the state of the industry.

Linie International - *www.linie-international.com*
A German lingerie magazine offering background information and
market analysis on lingerie, beachwear, nightwear and menswear.
Four publications are available each year.

Mody - *www.modaintymna.com.pl*
A Polish lingerie magazine, started in 1995, covers business trends and market analysis. Four publications each year.

Punto y Seguido - *www.revistapuntoyseguido.com*
A Spanish lingerie magazine established since 1996, an up-to-date view on the industry and new trends. Four publications each year.

Sous - *www.sous-magazin.ne*
A German trade lingerie magazine, covering mens and womens underwear, as well as beachwear and swimwear. Includes retail and trend reports. Four publications each year.

The best of Intima - *www.thebestofintima.com*
Founded in 2001, this US lingerie magazines covers new products, trends, and catwalk shows. Two publications a year.

Underlines - *www.underlinesmagazine.com*
Established in 1989, this UK magazine covers reports and forecasts of the intimate market and presents new collections from brands. Five publications each year.

FASHION MAGAZINES

Agenda - *www.agendamag.com*
Going since 2004, this is an online LA based fashion and lifestyle webzine, includes videos of runways, interviews with designers, and covers beauty, health and music.

Elle - *www.elleuk.com (UK) www.elle.com (Worldwide)*
Available in the UK and USA, covers fashion, celebrity news, trends, and reports from international collections.

Factio - *www.factio-magazine.com*
A Chicago based publication, covers fashion, art, beauty, culture and travel. Showcasing talented designers and international shows.

Fashion Insider - *www.fashioninsider.co.uk*
Available in a few selected places throughout the UK, France and Holland, but very much covers international fashion. Forward thinking in that you can interact via social media, it brings news of events around the globe so you can keep abreast of the latest trends.

Fashion Magazine - *www.fashionmagazine.com*
A Canadian based magazine, although primary based to bring fashion finds to designers in Canada, the magazine also covers international fashion.

Fashion Worlds - *www.fashionworlds.blogspot.com*
This blog examines designers and fashion from the past, with insights into present international designers. The blog is beautifully written, very insightful and explores fashion in a deeper social context.

Flip-zone - *www.flip-zone.com*
A french based company (on the website there is an option to view in English), features many collections of haute couture as well as ready to wear fashion.
Harper's Bazaar - *www.harpersbazaar.co.uk*
An elegant magazine; which contains outstanding photography, the magazine covers fashion, beauty, travel, culture and people.

Hint - *www.hintmag.com*
New York based, but covers global fashion, designers, models and parties from a unique perspective.

Iconique - *www.iconique.com*
An ezine; which features virtual catwalk shows and trends.

Japanese Streets   -   *www.japanesestreets.com*
A magazine which contains; street culture and catwalk fashion.

JC Report   -   *www.jcreport.com*
Founded in 2002, Jason Campbell delivers consistent cutting edge style reports, uncovering key trends and movements to an international audience.

Kurv Mag   -   *www.kurvmag.com.au*
An Australian high quality magazine; that is distributed three times a year. It delivers stylistic inspiration on fashion.

Nylon   -   *www.nylonmag.com*
An American magazine that concentrates on pop culture and fashion. It's name references New York and London.

Trendzine   -   *www.fashioninformation.com*
A fashion information service, that offers highly accurate trend predictions to the fashion industry.

Twill   -   *www.twill.info*
Dubbed the 'impossible' magazine, because it doesn't subscribe to trends or main stream fashion, it crosses boundaries with its artistic freedom.

Vogue   -   *www.vogue.co.uk*
An international fashion and lifestyle magazine, published in eighteen countries, corresponding directly to the fashion within that country.

FABRICS

Choosing fabric can not only lead you to your final idea, but can expand your original thoughts. Online and instore browing of shops or attending trade shows to pick up contacts of fabrics companies will give you a broader knowledge of the design you want to produce.

Charmeuse A man made skin like fabric

Chenille A soft fuzzy fabric made from short lengths of yarn called 'pilé'.

Chiffon An extremely sheer and lightweight material, made of highly twisted filament yarns.

Cotton A natural breathable fibre which is spun into yarn or thread.

Denier A unit or fineness based on a standard mass per length

Lace A delicate decorative fabric, woven in a web of different symmetrical patterns and figures. Available as an edge lace, an all over lace or a galloon lace.

Mesh An open-weave knitted or woven fabric, that has a net or sheer-look.

Microfibre Refers to synthetic fibres that measure less than one denier.

Modal Made from reconstituted cellulose from beech trees, is very soft and smooth.

Nylon A synthetic fibre known for it's flexibility, another name for nylon is now polyamide.

Polyester Is both the name of the fabric and fibre, great stretch ability and multidudes of usage.

Power Net A two-way stretch nylon fabric that provides excellent support.

Satin A woven fabric, that is highly lustrous on one side, and matte on the other.

Silk A natural protein fibre produced by the silkworm in the construction of its cocoon.

*The book The Anatomy of the Bra covers in detail where different fabrics are used on the bra and online suppliers.

Chapter Three

MARKET

What is Market Analysis?

A market analysis is the study and dynamics of a certain market in a certain industry. Through analyzing the market, the business strategies of your company can be identified.

http://en.wikipedia.org/wiki/Market_analysis

For example, if you decided to go into designing sports bras, by analyzing the market need; you would soon discover that there would be no point in designing around or buying netting for this garment as it would be too itchy and offer no support within the sports field.

Identifying your target market..

By identifying your target market, you can pitch your marketing, directly aiming at the right person. When you start to design you'll often find that your designs cater for a numerous amount of people; but all your hard work and designs will fail if you try to be everything to everybody. You will waste copious amounts of time and money trying to sell to everyone.

Choose a target market and then let your business grow from there. In order to reach your targeted consumer you have to know about them. This will then lead you to decide which direction you want your designs to head. This is also true for designing for other companies as well, you will need to know exactly what type of customer you are designing for, in order for your designs to work. As an example you would produce different designs for 'Agent Provocateur' than you would for 'Marks and Spencers'.

Trouble identifying your target market?

Sometimes it can be a bit overwhelming to identify your market, or you may simply think that you don't know your market and all you want to do is start designing. Remember every brand or label has a market. Whether that is working with certain fabrics, only designing for a certain size, or designing in a certain style. The aim is for your lingerie to be distinguishable.

If you have a million and one ideas buzzing around in your mind, sit down and decide which direction you are wanting to head. The key thing is to remember; never make your target market about price point. There will never be a way to compete with the chain stores, discover something else to offer your target market. Now is maybe the time to go online and look at other designers, and you'll see that by looking at their websites, all their designs are interlinked in one way or another. If you're still stuck, at the end of this book there are interviews with designers from numerous lingerie brands. Each have their own target market. Each different from one and another.

The direction of your brand.

When deciding which way you want to go with your label, there are important factors to consider.

1. Passion

Being passionate about your brand, is an important aspect. This is what you will rely on when you're working seven days a week, and over twelve hour days. Being passionate will carry you through when everything seems to be going 'tits up' and frustration appears - trust me it will occur at some point. In the long run, it's the passion that will sell your label brand to the buyer; your passion is what helps your brand grow.

2. Niche

Finding a niche in the market can help your brand. Designing for a niche market means you cut out some of your competitors. However, the down side would be that it may take you longer to grow your brand, as you are only covering a small segment of the market.

3. Style

As touched on previously, creating a strong style in your brand not only brings recognition; but it also brings trust from your customer. Keeping a customer is easier than gaining a customer. If you're designing delicate floral lingerie one month, then heavy sports inspired lingerie the next; you're going to confuse the customer and they will simply go elsewhere. Shoppers like to identify with a brand and relish in consistency. Get it right and customers can be very loyal. Word of mouth will be the best way to advertise your brand.

Keeping on track

Keeping on track can be one of the toughest parts of designing your own label. Especially each season you have to analyze what worked and what didn't. You are also surrounded by different fabrics and trends. It'll sometimes feel like you are being pulled in every direction. Keeping your target market in mind in these situations will help you keep on track.

One designer I worked with went a step further. After she worked out her target market she worked out the finer details and did a mock customer profile. Every time she was unsure of any design she looked at her customer profile to see if her mock customer would buy what she was designing. Something so simple has stopped her investing in buying random fabric, which personally she loved; but knew that the customers she already had and the ones she was trying to attract would be confused, as it didn't fit in with her brand.

It's not just about buying fabrics and components that this list can help you with, it can also steer you in the right direction on photo-shoots and marketing.

An example of her fifteen questions for her mock customer were are over the page.

1. Age bracket.
2. Earnings approx.
3. Where do you shop?
4. Where do you go out?
5. What car do you drive?
6. Where do you live?
7. What type of music do you like?
8. Ideal dream job?
9. Favourite drink (non alcoholic).
10. Favourite drink (alcoholic).
11. Celebrity you aspire to?
12. Three words to describe your personality.
13. Ideal way to spend a Saturday?
14. Fashion style.
15. Favourite classic fashion item.

* Remember, this wasn't a questionnaire she gave out to determine her customer requests. It was questions which she answered with her customers in mind, to gain a deeper insight and direction for which way she wanted her label to head.

Chapter Four

Sketch Books
& MOOD BOARDS

The Importance of a sketch book...

Whilst most designers will agree that keeping a sketch book is a great idea, its surprising how few actually do it. With the two main excuses being time and I can't draw.

** SKETCH BOOKS ARE NOT ABOUT BEING A GREAT DESIGNER THEY ARE ABOUT BEING A GREAT THINKER **

Sketchbooks can be filled with words, magazine tears, sketches, photos, generally anything that inspires you. It's these things that will lead your design process. You might already know what you want to design, but sketch books will help you in the future or to refine your ideas. That picture of the grey sofa with the oversized orange buttons you stuck in, could lead you to a whole new collection in the future. Don't be too precious about your sketchbook. Treat it like a brain-storming session, nothing has to make sense, nothing has to be neat;

and nothing has to be finished. The importance of it all, is to keep doing, keep going; as this is where you'll create your own style. With ideas being out of your head you can then fully concentrate on all the other mundane tasks that comes with being a designer. You will be able to go back to your designs later and build on them. It will make it easier in the future when you need to inspire yourself to move forward.

Sketch books are a personal thing, for some people the concept of a blank book is daunting (if this is the case, skip the first two pages so you don't feel pressured to come up with something astounding). Some people simply work best using single sheets of paper, back of envelopes, or digital media. As long as you have somewhere to store your ideas together, something that works for you. Sometimes hunting through for that one image you remember tearing out of a magazine but can't remember where it is, won't be time productive.

On the following pages are a couple of examples of sketchbook pages, both very different, including computer generated drawings, hand drawings, and inspirational magazine cuttings. None are right, none are wrong, none are perfect. They are just different ways of working.

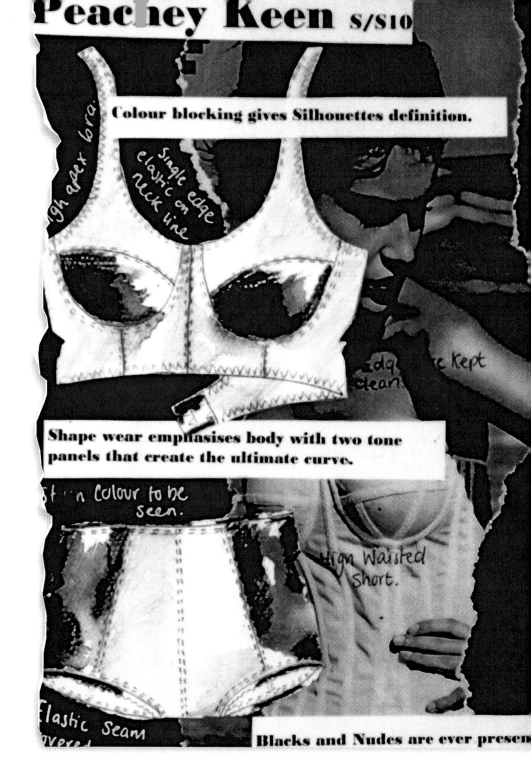

Peachey Keen S/S10

Colour blocking gives Silhouettes definition.

high apex bra.

single edge elastic on neck line

edge to be kept clean.

Shape wear emphasises body with two tone panels that create the ultimate curve.

in Colour to be seen.

High Waisted Short.

Elastic Seam covered.

Blacks and Nudes are ever presen

How to become a Lingerie Designer

Style of Mood Boards

Designers use mood boards to develop concepts and to communicate to others what direction of style they want to pursue. A mood board usually consists of images – photographs and/or sketches, colour samples, fabric swatches, and text. In short, mood boards serve as a visual tool to quickly inform others for the 'overall' feel of the design. Bear in mind that although creating mood boards in a digital form may be easier and quicker, a physical mood board tends to have a higher impact on people because of the more complete feeling that it offers.

Designing mood boards

The best results for an industry way of presenting mood boards, is to design digital mood boards, and if printing them out, attaching fabrics will make your work look professional.
You can either scan images from your sketch book or design your mood board on programmes such as Adobe Photoshop or Illustrator.

Below is a sample list of internet sites which can get help you create your mood board, there are many more you can search for, if none of the below provide you with what you need.

1. www.moodshare.co.uk
Moodshare allows you to make and share multi-user collaborative mood boards.

2. www.sampleboard.com
Sampleboard enables you to share visual ideas with clients.

3. www.atinytribe.com
An app for the ipad – the moodboard is a blank slate for your ideas; you can use your own ideas, or start with a pre-theme mood board.

4. www.beeclip.com
In two steps you create a mood boards – choose a mood board style then upload your pictures.

5. www.mural.ly
Mural.ly describes itself as 'Google Docs for visual people'. An easy and user-friendly way for creative teams to think, imagine and discuss their design ideas.

There is a great device that you can download to your computer and/or phone which can be synced, called 'evernote' (www.evernote.com) basically whatever note, reference or picture you are wanting for your mood board, 'evernote' will remember it and organize it for you. When you come back to images at a later date, you are not trawling through image after image. They have also introduced an Evernote notebook, which allows you to take a photo of the page and it transforms it digitally, so you can save it and it'll organise it, so again you're not flicking back through your notes to find that idea you jotted down when you were out. It really does make everything a lot quicker. If you are wanting to share your images, or want to be inspired by others 'Pinterest' (www.pinterest.com) lets you organize and share all the stunning images you find on the web. Their mission "is to connect everyone in the world through the 'things' they find interesting".

On the following pages are examples of mood boards. Again there is no right or wrong, if you're sketch book is strong, you can always scan in the page and use that. Sometimes one image is strong enough, another time maybe you want to go a step further and add fabrics or drawings etc. (Centre photo taken from a Sunday Times photoshoot).

MOOD: Drawing directly from the 1940's, lingerie is soft and sensual, with high waisted bloomers and unstructured bras. Lingerie tells the story of it's fabric authentically beginning it's life earlier. The lingerie identifies and enhances the women's femininity of that era.

Out of the Past

1940's

...and so she began to sew...

This page is a mood board for colours and styles of a season. The main picture is shot by Lara Jade, top right lingerie by Marlies Dekkers, middle right eye mask by Ma Mignonnette, bottom right lingerie by Bordello, and bottom left lingerie by Damaris.

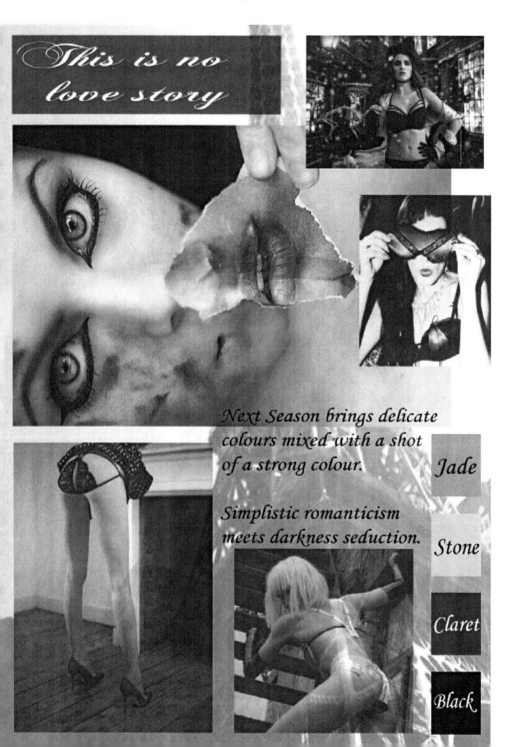

This is no love story

Next Season brings delicate colours mixed with a shot of a strong colour.

Simplistic romanticism meets darkness seduction.

Jade

Stone

Claret

Black

The next mood board was used as an example for colour, taking inspiration from the catwalks to lingerie.

Chapter Five

Fashion
DRAWINGS

Fashion drawing styles

Fashion drawings are used to represent the garment that you are going to design. Years ago they were more popular, gracing the cover of magazines such as Vogue (in the 1930s). Today they play a minor part in the communication of fashion. That said, fashion illustration can still serve as a beautiful form of art.

As the fashion model is only used to represent the garment, your own style can be refined for this. Although usually, designers just do a quick sketch of the design they want. Being able to actually translate your design onto figure drawings, will obviously be of help to you. If you have no samples and want to sell your lingerie or start to create a buzz about your brand.

It's worth noting that in over the thirteen years that I have been designing lingerie I have never once drawn a fashion figure, I've only sketched a garment by hand or CAD. However, employers may want to see that you draw, so although you may never need to actually figure draw your design, it's always best to hone in on your own style and practice so that you have a portfolio with designs, to prove you can do it.

Help with fashion drawings

Some people are blessed with the ability to draw fashion figures, whilst others need guidance in getting the proportions right. As a basic guide to drawing fashion figure, to make it look like a fashion figure you need to split the body of model five times (see picture on next page page) in proportion given and then trace round the model and thin your figure approximately 5mm, and this should give you a fashion figure template to work from.

There are websites which offer free templates for fashion figures.

1. www.fashion-era.com – covers silhouettes from different eras, basic half body and full body templates, also has an option to buy further fashion figures.

2. www.fashion-templates.com – offers free tutorials on drawing fashion figures and close up parts of the body.

3. www.designersnexus.com – a wide range of free fashion templates, each template is mirrored. Many have guidelines across the body so you can understand the principal of drawing a fashion figure.

How to become a Lingerie Designer

Fashion Drawings

Fashion drawings can be as detailed or as simple as you desire, depending on the final result you require. Never think there is a wrong or right style on fashion drawings, adapt and build on a style that most suits you and your brand.

Delicate Lace, goes across the back of the brief, with a bow CB.

ERIN

Lace runs down the front seam of the cup. Black bows sit at the base on the cradle.

The brief is rouched at center front leg to create a fifties shape. Bows are placed mid leg.

How to convert a Fashion Drawing to finished piece.

Lingerie Design

S/S'08

Mixing a vintage retro print, with modern brights. To create a surfery feel.

Chapter Six

Working
DRAWINGS
Importance of working drawings

A working drawing also known as a 'technical drawing' is the final construction of how the garment is going to look. It allows the designer, buyer or manufacturer to see how it will finally end up. Unlike the fashion figure that was art based, the working drawing is the technical version. Included in the working drawing usually are construction lines, button or bow placement, and stitch lines.

Working drawings are always drawn flat, never from an angle. These drawings are very important they will be the ones that convey your design to others if you intend to outsource. From these drawings a pattern maker and manufacturer will be able to work from them. When doing a working drawing, take it that the person you are sending to doesn't have any knowledge of the make-up of the garment. This will ensure that you draw or write all the information you need, even if you think it's glaringly obvious. Down to the last bar-tack.

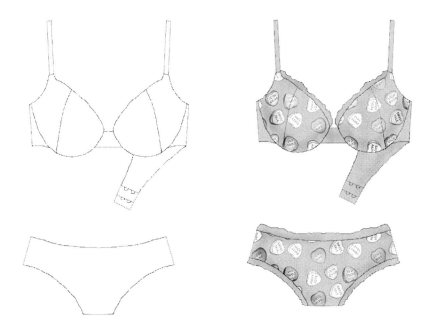

Working drawings can be done either by hand or computer. By computer you will be able to mirror the image easier, therefore give more of a professional finish.

Basic working drawings

Like basic fashion drawings, the working drawing becomes easier with practice. The following working drawings shown are basic working drawings. Once you have a working drawing it is easy to move them forward by adding colour, fabric prints, and sewing lines. I have included examples of starting points, with an outline, then adding fabric ideas. Also shown are of basic shapes of soft bras.

Outline working drawings with stitch detail and typical construction pieces.

Chapter Seven

Pattern books

In this book we shall only touch upon a basic pattern for the brief and bra. Those who want to learn more about patterns, www.pattern-school.com is a blog aimed specifically at teaching students of fashion design, how to make close-fit, stretch-wear patterns. For further information if you want to have an insight on which pattern books to buy it also gives an insight and review of the following books.

- Metric Pattern Cutting by *Winifred Aldrich*
- Shirt Making by *David Page Coffing*
- Pattern Cutting for Lingerie, Beach & Leisurewear by *Ann Hagar*
- Design and Patternmaking for Stretch Fabrics by *Keith Richardson*
- Making Beautiful Bras by *Lee-Ann Burgess*
- The Bra Makers Manuel by *Beverly Johnson*
- Dress Pattern Designing by *Natalie Bray*
- Knitting Lingerie Style by *Joan McGowan-Michael*
- High Fashion Sewing Secrets by *Claire B. Shaeffer*
- Pattern Making - A comprehensive Reference for Fashion Design by *Sylvia Rosen*
- The Entrepreneur's Guide to Sewn Product Manufacturing by Kathleen Fasanella

The history of patterns

A pattern is a paper or cardboard template, from which the parts of a garment are traced onto fabric before cutting out and assembling (sometimes called paper patterns).

Pattern making or pattern cutting is the art of designing patterns. A custom-fitted basic pattern, from which patterns for many different styles can be created is called a sloper or block.

Four historic American pattern companies still exist:

Butterick | *McCall's* | *Simplicity* | *Vogue*

Ebeneezer *Butterick* in 1863 changed the face of home sewing as we know today, from a conversation with his wife whilst she made their baby son an outfit. She wished you could get patterns already sized for the size you wanted. At that point you could only buy a one size pattern, and had to grade it yourself (make it bigger or smaller). Ebeneezer a tailor himself considered her idea, and shipped out patterns on tissue paper with instructions on how to make up the garment. Butterick's patterns became available to the public and his business grew to the extent that in 1904 he was receiving an average of 29,762 letters each week with questions, suggestions and ideas.

Typical pattern
packaging from
Mcalls and
Simplicity

James *McCall* a Scottish tailor, established the 'McCall Pattern Company' in 1870 in New York City. He began designing and printing his own sewing patterns and founded a magazine 'The Queen' in which the patterns were available. The patterns were blank until 1919, then they began printing information directly onto the pattern pieces. McCall usually printed the date of release on their envelopes (the only company which consistently did so before mid-century).

Simplicity Pattern started producing patterns in 1927. Their goal was to produce an easy-to-use, lower-priced pattern. Patterns were blank until 1946. They embarked on a major sewing education program where by fashion shows, educational books and literature were presented by travelling representatives.

Vogue Patterns began in 1899, as a weekly feature in Vogue Magazine. The patterns could be purchased for 50 cents, though they were only available in size 36, (bust measurement). Vogue Pattern Company was formed in 1914, and in 1916 Vogue patterns were sold in department stores. In 1961 Butterick licensed the name and began to produce patterns under the Vogue name.

In 2001 The McCall Pattern Company acquired Butterick and Vogue Patterns. Where along with McCall's patterns it continues to offer the most advanced, high quality patterns, catalogues, and magazines to keep up with the changing needs of fashion.

How to create a pattern

A designer usually employs one of three pattern creation methods:

1 Flat-pattern method: which begins with a slope or block. This basic pattern is refined by making a mock up garment (a toile). From fitting the garment, alterations are then made, when you are happy with the garment, a pattern is then taken from the toile.

2 Drafting method: this is most likely to be used in menswear design. It involves drafting a pattern directly onto pattern paper using a variety of straight edges and curves.

3 Draping method: this is used for more elaborate designs that are hard to obtain through the flat pattern method. This is because it's near impossible to know how the fabric will drape or hang without actually doing a 3-dimensional test run. To use this method it involves pinning fabric onto a dress form (dummy). Then transferring the fabric with all it's markings onto a paper pattern, or using the fabric as the pattern itself.

On the following pages is how to make a pattern of the brief that is shown in the pictures. This method starts with a grid box and then an X Y axis are measured.

You will never be asked to produce a pattern in the method displayed on the following pages. This method will just enable you to have a pattern to start from.Tracing the patterns from a piece of lingerie is probably the quickest method, then starting from that base you can manipulate it to build up your own reference of patterns.

The simplest way to do a pattern is to start with a garment that you know fits, and adjust it. If you want to take a plain brief and make it into a boy style brief, simply add a line at mid thigh point, angled up to the waist and cut down that line, then add a seam allowance on to each side.

*Remember whatever style line you add into a basic pattern, you need to add a seam allowance to each new side of the pattern this avoids making your pattern smaller.

Using the same pattern

Pictures of briefs using the pattern that your about to be shown. You can see in the bottom picture that the material had more stretch so the side seams appear deeper and the rise (from the gusset to the top of the brief) is higher.

From this pattern, you can see that by adding a couple of style lines you can alter the style of the brief without too much work, yet completely alter the look. The picture below shows the front of the pattern has been altered, a style line was inserted at the mid leg point.

Just by changing the back of the brief, you get another completely different look.

The brief style could also be altered by changing the fabric of the top or bottom piece of the brief. Showing that you do not have to make endless patterns, simply changing the trims, fabric or adding new style lines means you have numerous amount of designs.

·* Keep things simple for yourself * ·

Making a brief block pattern

Making a brief block pattern
We are going to cover one method to make a size medium basic brief pattern; by hand. The pattern will consist of three pieces – front, back and gusset piece.

To make the pattern by hand you will need.

Graph or square paper
Pencil and pen
Set square or long ruler
French Curve,

(or a very steady hand!)

Front Brief

In order to make sure both sides are exactly the same, you will be working on only one side. If you're paper is big enough fold it in half, if not fold the fabric in half and place the pattern edge on the fold so you get a complete brief piece.

Draw a rectangle 22cm across and 28 cm down.

There are 15 measurements to be marked out. We are going clockwise starting from the top. (Gusset measurements are stated on the next couple of pages).

1. $X = 0$ $Y = 26.5$
2. $X = 7$ $Y = 27$
3. $X = 14$ $Y = 27.5$
4. $X = 19.5$ $Y = 28$
5. $X = 22$ $Y = 19.5$
6. $X = 14$ $Y = 19$
7. $X = 11.5$ $Y = 18.5$
8. $X = 8.5$ $Y = 17.5$
9. $X = 6.5$ $Y = 15.5$
10. $X = 4.5$ $Y = 12.5$ (put a notch mark here as this is where your gusset comes to).
11. $X = 4$ $Y = 11.5$
12. $X = 3.5$ $Y = 7$
13. $X = 4$ $Y = 3$
14. $X = 4.5$ $Y = 0$
15. $X = 0$ $Y = 0$

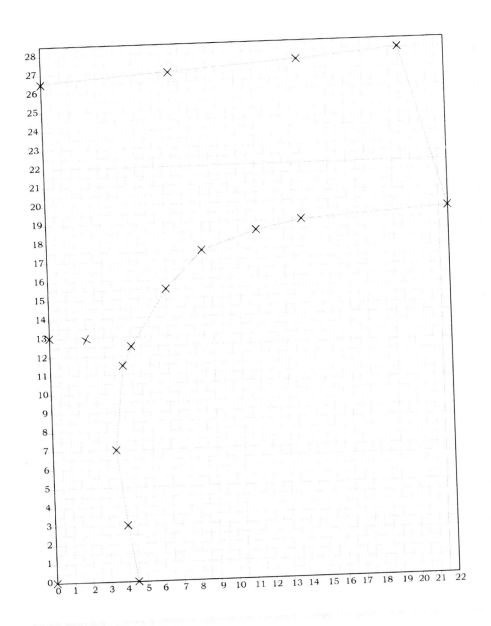

How to become a Lingerie Designer

Information on a pattern

Next you need to mark the pattern. You can write your seam allowance on it, but most factories will work to the standard.

Information you need on the pattern is:

1. What the pattern is
2. Size
3. Pattern number or reference
4. How many need to be cut
5. Selvedge (*or if this pattern is for you and you will be using it for different fabrics, just note down the stretch so you can apply this to every fabric*).
6. Type of fabric to be used

The selvedge of the fabric is the two edges of the roll; you need this so you know which way to lay the pattern. Diagonal to the selvedge is called the bias.

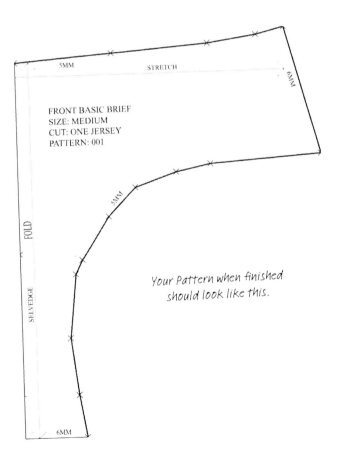

FRONT BASIC BRIEF
SIZE: MEDIUM
CUT: ONE JERSEY
PATTERN: 001

Your Pattern when finished should look like this.

Gusset Pattern

(See previous front brief pattern)
I have left the outline of the brief so you know how the gusset sits in correlation to the front of the brief.
There are eight measurements for this piece; it is exactly the same shape as the bottom part of the brief.

1. X = 0   Y = 13
2. X = 2   Y = 13
3. X = 4.5   Y = 12.5
4. X = 4   Y = 11.5
5. X = 3.5   Y = 7
6. X = 4   Y = 3
7. X = 4.5   Y = 0
8. X = 0   Y = 0

Your Pattern when finished should look like this.

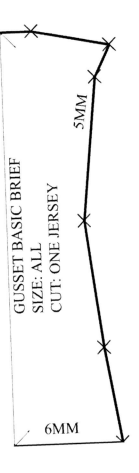

GUSSET BASIC BRIEF
SIZE: ALL
CUT: ONE JERSEY
5MM
6MM

Back Brief

Measure out a rectangle measuring 22cm across and 28.5cm down. There are 13 measurements that you need to mark down. The measurements will be starting from the top and going round in a clockwise direction, (as with all measurements, the X measurement will come first then the Y).

1. $X = 0$ $Y = 21.5$
2. $X = 20$ $Y = 22.5$
3. $X = 22$ $Y = 13.5$
4. $X = 19.5$ $Y = 13$
5. $X = 18$ $Y = 12.5$
6. $X = 15$ $Y = 11$
7. $X = 13$ $Y = 9.5$
8. $X = 11$ $Y = 8$
9. $X = 9$ $Y = 6$
10. $X = 7$ $Y = 3.5$
11. $X = 5.5$ $Y = 1.5$
12. $X = 4.5$ $Y = 0$
13. $X = 0$ $Y = 0$

Joining the dots up with your ruler and French curve, your pattern should look like this: (next page)

Back Brief Pattern

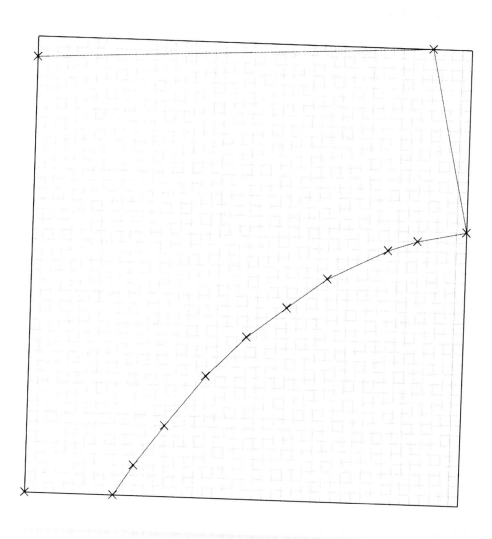

Complete Basic Brief Pattern

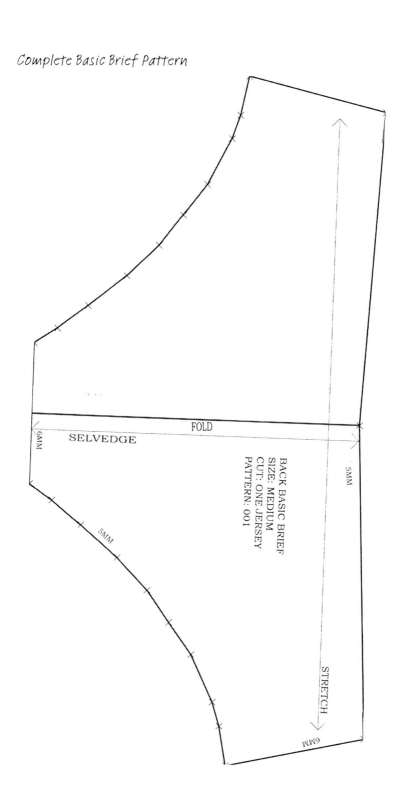

FOLD

6MM

SELVEDGE

5MM

5MM

BACK BASIC BRIEF
SIZE: MEDIUM
CUT: ONE JERSEY
PATTERN: 001

STRETCH

6MM

Chapter Eight

Bra PATTERNS

Soft bra

A soft cup bra is the easiest bra style to design and make. You do not have to worry about fitting the cup around a wire. When designing a soft bra don't feel restricted to the shape, you can push the boundaries. By altering the height of the apex (the top of the bra) or make the cup, seamed, darted, gathered, etc. You may want to begin with soft cup bras until you get more confident about underwired bras. Most women wear underwired bras so depending on what market you are aiming for, will dictate what type of bra you are going to design.

Pattern pieces of a bra

An underwired bra usually falls into two categories, with or without a cradle. Take a look at some bras. If they have a cradle the centre front piece and the wing will meet; forming a cradle under the cup.
If the bra does not have a cradle them it will simply have a centre front piece, attached to the front side of the cup and a wing attached to the side of the cup; these will not meet.

Examples of Cradle Bras using the same Pattern:

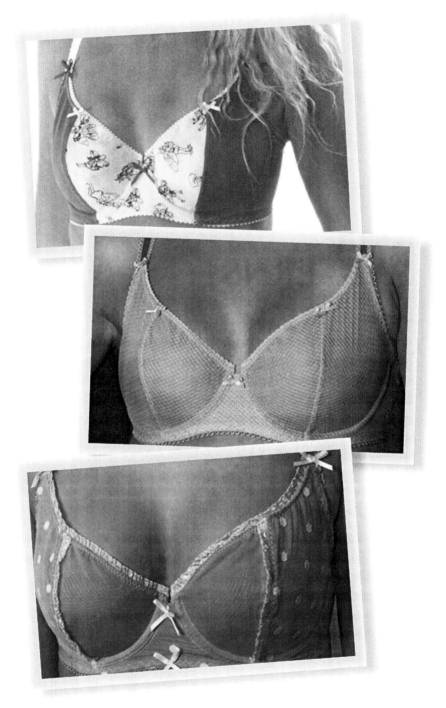

Examples of non-cradle bras using the same pattern:

A bra will usually consist of three main pieces, the cup, the wing, and the centre front (can be known as centre gore).

The Cup
Depending on what size bra you are designing, the cup can come in many different piece variations:

- Darted.
- A two piece cup with a vertical seam, so you have a side cup piece and front cup piece.
- A two piece cup with a horizontal seam, so you have a top cup piece and bottom cup piece.
- A 'three piece' cup; which has a horizontal seam, so you will have a top cup piece, but the bottom piece cup is split with a vertical seam, so you have a bottom cup front piece, and a bottom cup side piece.

The 'three piece' cup is usually designed for women with larger breasts, as breaking the cup into more pattern pieces creates more volume and will give a better shape for women. Creating a pattern piece with curved edges will create more volume.

The Wing
This is the part which goes round the body; it meets at the back of the body with the hook and eye. It can be made from the same fabric as the cup but it's mainly made from power net. The stronger the power net, the more secure a fit the bra will be; which is something to consider as 85% of the support should come from the under band not the straps. If you want to design a great fitting bra, regardless of what size you are designing for then think about the wings. All too often these can be an after thought. For example changing the way the straps are attached at the back of the bra to the wing can get minimize the 'back fat' that women complain about. As a result of this many women opt to wear a bigger sized bra so they don't suffer. It's not the size they have got wrong it's the style of the bra. Most bras, especially on the high street will have the back strap going directly into the

wing, (this is usually a cheaper manufacturer method). Technically this style is a called a camisole strap. Larger cup bras will have the bra elastic going from the hook and eye, up to the back strap. Which is technically called a leotard strap. This allows for the wings to be wider when it meets the cup, creating an even distribution of the weight of the breasts.

The Centre Front
The centre front is much like the 'key stone' on an arch of a bridge, it holds the bra together and carries the majority of stress of the bra. The centre front should never be made from stretch fabrics alone, stabilizer is put behind the centre front so it doesn't stretch.

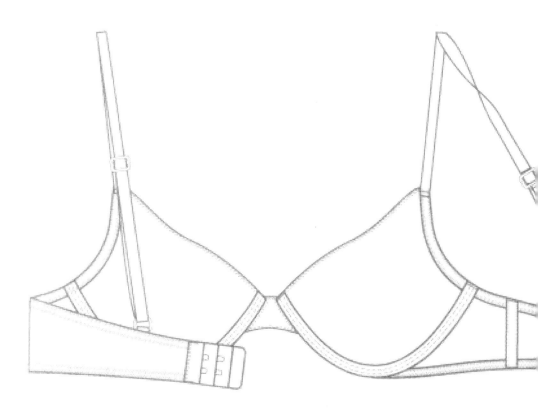

The Bra Wire

When designing an underwired bra always design around the bra wire. This is the component which gives you support, so designing around it is important. You can find the wires natural balance point by placing it on a table with the wires sticking up in the air. There will be a point in which it will naturally stay. This point is also where your wing and centre front should meet if your designing a bra with a cradle.

If you want to take a pattern off your existing bra, I recommend taking the wire out first then trying to take a rough pattern off the bra, then unpicking it. This is because all too often whilst unpicking, the fabric can fray or parts may get chopped off.

If you are designing a bra with a cradle, a quick way to see if you have the right shape is to lay your wire on top of the pattern. The top side of the wing (where it will sit under the arm) should be roughly 1.5cm away from the wire. This is to allow for the natural spring of the wire when it's worn in order to give support.

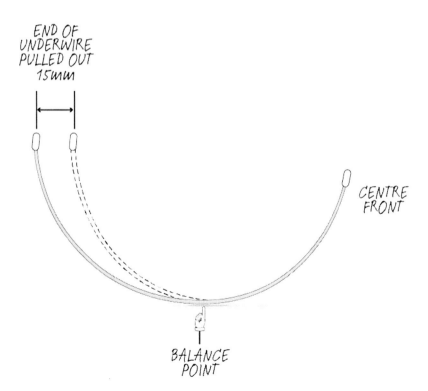

Components of a Bra

Other items you need to consider when designing your bra are,

The hook and eye,
Bra strapping,
Rings and Slides,
Elastic to go on the wings
Elastic to go on the top of the cup (or lace).

For those who are wanting more detail about the component of the bra, please refer to the book 'The Anatomy of the Bra', which breaks down each component into great detail.

Avaialable on Kindle
and in Paperback

Chapter Nine

Specification
SHEETS

What is a Spec sheet?

Specification sheets or 'Spec sheets' as they are known, provide all the information that takes a pattern into a finished garment. Spec sheets are designed to include technical detailed diagrams, construction notes, garment measurements, label placements, fabric and trim details. Each company has their own format, but the information is the same and is just tailored to the company needs. Learning how to measure clothing will be one of most important skills you can have.

Why use Spec sheets?

Spec sheets are the communication between the design team, technical team and factory. They help prevent costly errors, and ensure that the technical team understands exactly what the designer has in mind.

What goes on a Spec sheet?

Most often, at the top of the spec sheet will be information about your products, such as company name, logo, description, and style code. The spec sheet must also have key measurements, as well as dimensions of the garment in different standard sizes.

Important information such as bow placement is also needed, along with a sketch of the garment. Everything about the garment should be covered, such as thread colour, type of fabric, cuttings of fabrics and trims. Though this information may be found in 'Technical Packs' for some companies. It's helpful to send off your spec sheet before you send the garment off to be made, this can erase certain errors. Finally, the spec sheet should be sent with one of the seal samples of the garment so manufacturers know exactly what they are working towards.

A seal sample is a sample of the final garment; this sample should represent what the final piece should look like exactly. In some companies a seal sample may have a tag on it, to identify it, (usually a red or gold tag).

Measuring a 'brief' for a spec sheet.

The key measurements in a Spec sheet for a brief are:

1. Waist Relaxed - *Lying waist flat*
2. Waist Extended - *Waist stretched*
3. Front Rise - *Bottom seam to top of waist in the middle*
4. Back Rise - *Bottom seam to top of back waist in the middle*
5. Gusset Length - *Length of gusset*
6. Front Gusset Width - *Top of gusset – sometimes narrowest part of gusset is also measured*
7. Back Gusset Width - *Seam where front back and gusset is joined*
8. Side Seam Length - *Side of brief along seam*
9. ½ Leg Relaxed - *Leg flat*
10. ½ Leg Extended - *Leg stretched*

See the key measurements below

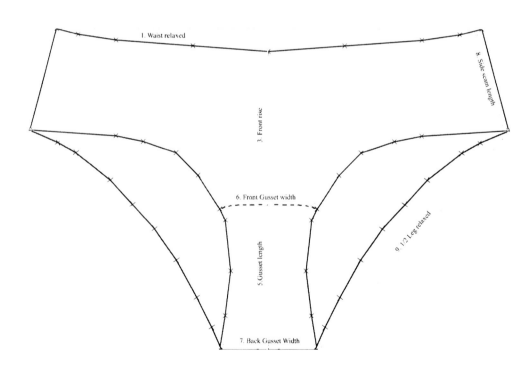

Measurements for a brief

The easiest and quickest way for future work is to produce your spec sheet on a 'spread sheet', where you can enter the values of how much you want each size to increase or decrease by. Each company will work to their own grading system. Most high street companies that I have worked for use the basic grading system.

These measurements go from sizes, Small to Large (but would be the same for sizes 8-14). Sizes above or below these require measurement changes along both the side and gusset seam, usually graded at 0.5cm

1. ½ Waist Relaxed: 2.5cm
2. ½ Waist Extended: 2.5cm
3. Front Rise: 1cm
4. Back Rise: 1cm
5. Gusset Length: 0cm
6. Front Gusset Width: 0cm
7. Back Gusset Width: 0cm
8. Side Seam Length: 0cm
9. ½ Leg Relaxed: 1.4cm
10. ½ Leg Extended: 1.4cm

The extended measurement is what you should be able to stretch it do, to ensure that it fits on the body. With the extended measurement I have kept it simple by implying that reducing the waist by 2.5 the stretch should do the same. Buyers and designers still work like this, however to get your correct technical stretch measurement, the stretch measurement would be the waist measurement relaxed x1.5 and the leg measurement relaxed x1.3.

This way takes into account the stretch ratio of the elastic. For example, reducing a 10cm piece of elastic of 5cm won't make it stretch 5cm smaller, it will still stretch the same ratio as the 10cm piece of elastic but just on a 5cm scale.

For those just starting out it's perfectly fine to just keep to the simple extended formula, as this still gets used a great deal.

A basic format of an Excel spreadsheet
Permission is given to use the layout and information of the spec sheet below.

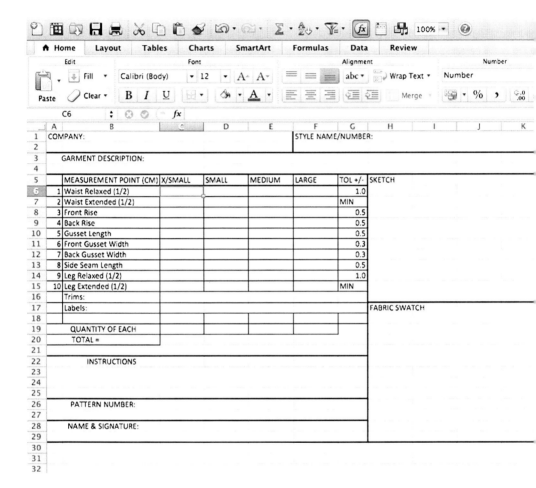

You can copy the idea into Excel yourself and formulize the spec sheet; so it increases or decreases the sizes to correspond to your sample size, this saves you work in the future.

I use the sample size medium as my starting point. Once having made your medium sample size, measure up your garment and enter the measurements into your database accordingly. In Excel after entering all your information click on the box of the Large measurement i.e. the waist measurement. You can see which box you are entering data into from the darker shaded letter at the top of the screen. This also corresponds with the number down the left hand side and will show in the far left hand small box at the top of the screen.

In the longer box at the top where you write all the information in, you need to enter = (equals takes the text into a formula, you will see where it once had what letter and number box you were on, it now has the word Sum). Enter = letter + number of the Medium measurement eg E6 +2.5 this will take whatever number you have in E6 (which is the Medium measurement) and automatically add 2.5. So if you had 28.1 in the Medium waist box, 30.6 should appear in the Large waist box.

With the Small it's just reversed so the formula is =E6-2.5 then you can right click copy and paste in the x/small box. Where the measurements stay the same for example the gusset length. Whatever measurement you enter in your sample size will stay the same for the rest of the sizes.

(Help with Excel formulas can be found by either entering your question in the 'Help' category at the top of the Excel page, or there is numerous websites on the matter).

When you have all the measurements the factory will know what size the garment should be coming up at. Tolerances are given for the factory to work towards, so each garment comes out the same size, with little discrepancies. As a rough guide in lingerie, 8cm and below would have a 3mm tolerance (some companies use 5mm), 8cm to 20cm would have a 5mm tolerance and 20cm above would have 1cm tolerance.

The spec sheet is there so you know that you have all the sizes coming up the correct size and that any 'Small' from your range will measure the same.

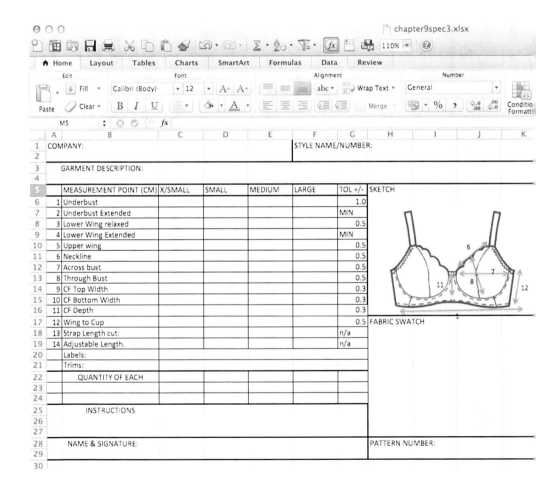

Measuring a 'Soft bra' for a spec sheet.

The key measurements in a spec sheet for a soft bra are:

1. **Underbust** - The measurement of the underband from hook to eye
   (*The hook & eye are not included in this measurement*)
2. **Underbust Extended** - The stretched measurement of the underband
3. **Lower Wing Relaxed** - The bottom of the wing lying flat
4. **Lower Wing Extended** - The stretch measurement of the wing lying flat.
5. **Upper Wing** - The top of the wing.
6. **Neckline** - The top of the cup.
7. **Across Bust** - From the centre front to the wing.
8. **Through Bust** - The middle of the cup top to bottom.
9. **CF Top Width** - The top of the centre front.
10. **CF Bottom Width** - The bottom of the centre front
11. **CF Depth** - The depth of the centre front.
12. **Wing to Cup** - Where the cup meets the wing.
13. **Strap Length cut** - The length in which the strap is cut.
14. **Adjustable Length** - The length in which you want your straps adjusted to

*Please note that on each bra you may not use all the measurements, it will depend on the style.

Key Measurements for an Underwire Bra

For underwire bras you have the same measurements, but you would also have:

15. **Outer edge of wire casing** - measuring the outer edge of the wire casing
16. **Underarm** - Measuring from the apex (where the strap meets the cup) along the underarm to the wing.

Measurements for a soft bra

These measurements are based on grading of sizes **Small, Medium & Large** as an example.

1. Underbust: 5cm
2. Underbust Extended: 5cm
3. Lower Wing Relaxed: 1.5cm
4. Lower Wing Extended: 1.5cm
5. Upper Wing: 1.5cm
6. Neckline: 1cm
7. Across Bust: 1cm
8. Through Bust: 1cm
9. CF Top Width: 0cm
10. CF Bottom Width: 0cm
11. CF Depth: 0cm
12. Wing to Cup: 0.5cm
13. Strap Length cut: 0cm
14: Adjustable Length: 0cm

Underwire Bra Measurements

Underwire bra specification differs depending on whether you are using moulded cups or a wire, as the patterns and grades are determined by this factor. If you are designing underwire bras without padding, each wire will have a grade. For example the difference between a 34B wire and a 34C wire could be 1.8cm, which means the base of the cup will follow this grade. Each size around the wire casing will increase by 1.8cm. If you're using a molded cup, the factory will provide you the size difference of each cup.

Chapter Ten

Grading

What is grading?

Grading is a skill; it involves using the master pattern piece and moving it according to the grading rules. Measurements are pre-determined by the company you are working for. The pattern will increase or decrease size but still retain the proportion of the original master pattern depending on the grading system. The grading measurements used here are the same used in the previous spec sheet. These are standard High Street measurements. Understanding the technical side of designing is one of the most important things you can accomplish. Knowing how patterns fit together and being able to create different sizes of the same garment will help you understand future designs.

Basic hand grading is usually done by moving the pattern; a ninety degree angle up and across. The grade will be done using X and Y references. Using normal hand grading rules –the X is horizontal and Y is vertical.

The more you understand about how different departments work the easier it is for you as a designer. Computer grading allows more options, by grading a line, and angles, rather than relying on grading on the X and Y axis.

The following grades I am going to show you are only one method. We will be moving the pattern up (Y axis) and out (X axis). Once you understand this you can then apply a grade by splitting the pattern so all your movement doesn't just grade on one part of the pattern.

As said at the start of this book, to gain a proper understanding of grading, I would advise buying a book solely on grading or attend a grading workshop. Once you master the basics you can apply the rules to complicated designs.

Using the information from the spec sheet, we know that with each size, the brief goes up by 1cm and out by 1.25cm (on the half).

We're going to keep things easy by putting the grade all in one direction, but it can be more technical and the grade can be spread equally throughout the pattern - by splitting the grade and grading both up and down.

Using the centre front on your brief, a line is drawn horizontally. Grade lines are drawn from this, 1cm above the horizontal line and 1.25 across from the centre front.

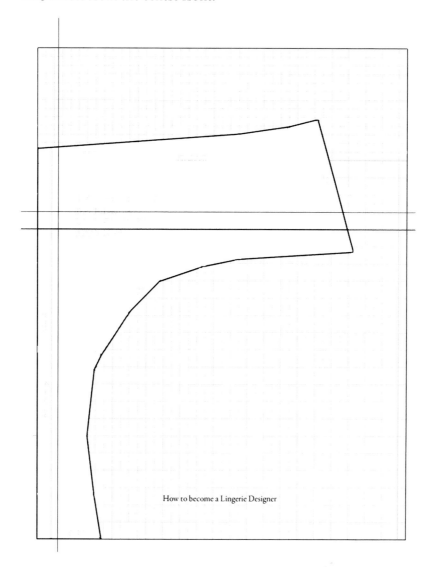

How to become a Lingerie Designer

Physically move the pattern up and across marking a point at your edges, this is your basic grade to a bigger size.

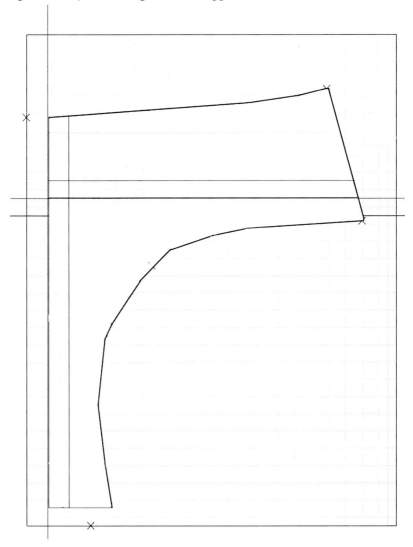

When comparing patterns (nested) to one another they should look as below. The back is graded the same way and from reading the spec sheet you know that the gusset does not have a grade value on it, it follows the front of the brief. The easiest thing to do is to make a replica copy of the front brief for the gusset.

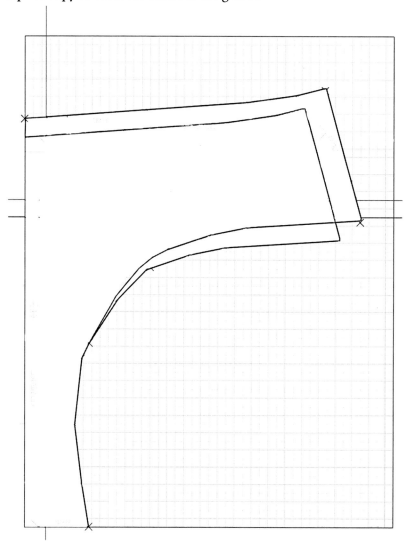

Understanding bra grading

It is no co-incidence that most designers start out designing soft bras in A –C cup. These can contain as little as 16 components whereas as an average underwire bra can contain up to 32 components plus. If you have no previous knowledge of underwired bras, you need to understand that you can't just grade up to bigger cups of D cup and above without doing a couple of tweaks to the measurements.

It is important to remember that the cup size and band size work together, i.e. the wearer of a 32C cup has a smaller bust than a 34C cup wearer. Someone wearing a 36B is wearing the same cup capacity as someone wearing a 30DD. Confused? You're not the only one. This is why so many women wear the wrong size bra. Welcome to the cross grading system.

Cross grading a bra

Cross grading a bra is when a 34B has the same cup size as a 32C and 30D, however the 32C has a smaller back. This is where most women go wrong when wearing a bra. Women usually have the right cup size, but the back of the bra rises up. By going down a band size and up a cup size, you are technically wearing the same cup size but the bra will fit better.

It is this size confusion that causes women heartache, having always worn a B cup they often don't want to hear that they should be wearing a D, even if technically it's the same size. Also you need to note that with the under bands, it usually goes the other way, so a 34B under band will be the same length as 32A under band and a 36C under band.

This table should help; all the bra sizes diagonally adjacent are technically the same cup size. The ones with no line in between are also technically the same cup size. For example, a 28E, 30DD, 32D, 34C, 36B and 38A all have the same cup capacity.

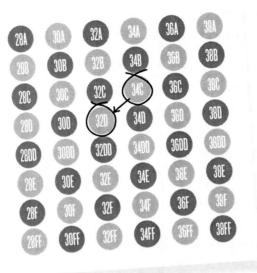

Grading a bra

If you are considering grading above a D cup, I strongly recommend that you seek out a professional grader who understands and has knowledge on bra grading. When working above a D cup you are dealing with more volume and standard cross grading won't cut it. Each new cup size should be taken as the base size for your next size up, unlike briefs where you can start with a Small and just keep grading to a Large. When grading bras from a D cup to a DD cup you will use the DD cup as your base size to grade to an E cup.
It is important to get bra grading right, for example if you're out 6mm that can mean you're into the next cup size. (See next page for when not to use the standard grade).

When grading you need to split the grade across the cup. If the cup increases by 1cm and you have a top and bottom piece cup then you need to increase the top and bottom piece of each piece by 0.25cm, not 0.5cm on one piece and 0.5cm on the other. Think of your pattern similar to when you drop a pebble in water, the circle of ripples expand outwards all at once, one side is not greater than the other.

When not to use the standard grade.

Standard grading cannot be used when it comes to larger cup sizes. Standard bra grading is un-dimensional, and takes no account of breast size, droop, shape, height, or width. Breasts over a certain cup size (also depending on the back size) have totally different shapes and drop etc. to the core size breast.

This is why so many companies that start out supplying smaller size lingerie and want to expand to cover the larger size cup market fail, because they haven't taken into account the different grading needed to supply the larger cup market.

For example if you applied the standard grade to a B cup and graded it up to an F cup the apex of the bra (the point at which the straps are attached to at the front) would be too wide for the wearers shoulders. With each grade for the larger cup market, the apex would need to be moved in towards the centre of the body by a couple of mm with each grade.

If you are looking to design bigger sizes, it's worth paying someone with years experience to make up your spec sheet and then get it graded professionally. Starting with a great fit for the 'larger cup size market' is what will keep your customers loyal.

Chapter Eleven

Sample SPEC SHEETS

What are sample spec sheets?

Sample sheets are what you as the designer fill in for the sample machinist to use. This allows the sample machinist to accurately sample up your garment. Samples should be in the correct fabric, for either the buyer to know what they are going to receive or for fit purposes. If you're just mocking up a sample to see how it fits together, then making a sample in an alternative fabric is acceptable. If this is the case always go for a pale fabric so that it allows you to write on it any changes you need to make. Sometimes if the garment is complicated you may make several samples before you get the correct pattern.

What to put on the Sample Sheet

When writing a sample sheet one of the most important part is the sketch. A hand drawn sketch is fine, a computer sketch is better; a technical sketch is better still.

A technical sketch is where you actually map out the measurements onto the computer sketch. (Like on your spec sheet). Even if you are planning to make the lingerie yourself the quicker you start to understand sample sheets and make them; the quicker it will be when you start to outsource your manufacturer. You can use your spec sheet as your sample spec sheet if you like. But make sure you write in if you have any special make up of the garment.

If you are using your spec sheet, you only need to include the measurements of the size you are using as your sample size. If you don't know the full sizes put 'TBC' (to be confirmed) in the measurements that you don't know. If your measurements are an approximation or a rough guide put that in your instruction box; so the sample machinist is not struggling to achieve the exact thing.

Don't forget to include:

1. Date
2. Description of garment
3. Style name or number
4. Pattern number you used
5. Any key measurements
6. Thread colour
7. Placement of bows and labels
8. Fabric swatch
9. Special make-up advice

Try and be as precise as possible, write like the sample machinists has never seen this piece of lingerie before; then you'll be sure to cover everything that you need to make up your sample.

Chapter Twelve

How important is understanding costing?

Costing a garment is one of the most valuable things you can understand about design. There have been many occasions when working for the high streets, when the garment has been received well but it was too expensive to be put into production. So it's back to the drawing board to alter it. Changing the style, fancy seams, linings, and trims or decorative stitching will decrease the cost.

Costing with bigger companies

If you're working for a big company, the costing sheet will look very different from the one seen here. Their costing will look similar to a spec sheet with a picture of the garment, measurements, and break down of costs which will include how much it takes for each sewing operation and what machine was used for the operation. For example to cross-stitch elastic on a garment is more expensive than to seam cover elastic on. This is because it's a longer machine operation.

The cost sheet should be detailed enough so that another person is able to order all the fabric and trims. It will include all the company names of where the fabric, trims, etc. come from and also the quantity of how much it takes to make the garment.

The costing sheet shown here just covers the basics. On the 'costing sheet' provided there should usually be a quote from the factory, measurements, names of the companies, and price of trims or fabrics. This gives you a basic idea of how much it should cost you to make the garment. Be aware though this costing sheet doesn't take into account overheads such as heat and electricity, labels, postage, threads, swing tickets, packaging, design research, markdown sale losses, advertising, and everything that goes along with owning a business including your time.

All of these factors have to be priced into your costing but shall be different for each garment and each company.

Measuring the elastics to cost

Before you can cost you need to measure your garment and also work out how much fabric and trims are being used.

Always measure a size that is in the middle of the size range. This will take into consideration the smaller and bigger size, for example if you have four sizes measure the bigger size of the middle one as a guide. For the elastics, measure (in metres or whatever unit you are buying elastic in) the waist and legs (if the same elastic) of the already made up briefs and enter the amount in the amount box.

Measuring fabrics to cost.

For the fabric you need to know how many pattern pieces you can fit on one metre of your chosen fabric. Companies will have a computer to do this, pattern cutters will move the pattern pieces onto a lay for the fabric to be cut taking into account fabric allowance. Doing it by hand with your pattern piece, either measure out one metre of your chosen fabric and lay the pieces on to see how many pieces; or measure out on paper or card a rectangle measuring one metre by the width of your fabric. Mark the selvedge on the paper, draw round the pattern pieces. Sometimes it's easier to work out how many pattern pieces will fit on one metre of the fabric, rather than try and fit them all on.

As a guide work out how many front pieces of the brief fit on the metre then how many back pieces. (See example over the page).

Once finding out your measurements, you can enter that number in the amount box, the cost (in metres) in the cost box and multiply these together to get the total cost of that part of the garment. This will let you know exactly how much each part of the brief will cost. Then you add it all up at the end. I have included multiple units so you know how much it will cost you for example 10, 20 and 100 units.

Be sure when you order your fabric to allow for wastage this could be from faults in the fabric, to manual faults when manufacturing occurs.

This is a very basic way but an easy way to help you start to understand how to do costs. Bigger companies all do their fabric usage on a computer using a grading package such as Geber, Lectra or Assyst.

This picture is not to scale, but gives you an example of how to lay the patterns; you may well have space at the end of the width of fabric (as shown in picture). This would be a place where you could put the gusset if you were using a self-fabric gusset or maybe bra patterns if you were making a bra to match.

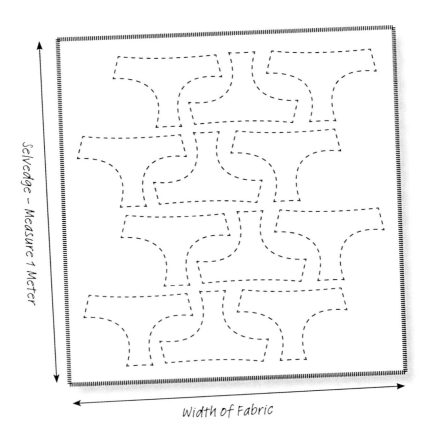

COMPANY:

GARMENT DESCRIPTION:

STYLE NAME/NUMBER:

COMPONENT	AMOUNT (M)	COST (£)	TOTAL (£)	SUPPLIER	CODE	10 UNITS	20 UNITS	100 UNITS
Elastic	1.8	0.05	0.09	blk frill supplier	00001	0.90	1.80	9.00
Elastic	n/a							
TRIMS								
Bow: 1 xGreen at CF	1	0.01	0.01	bow supplier	045 green	0.10	0.20	1.00
Bow: 1 xpink at CB	1	0.01	0.01	bow supplier	011 pink	0.10	0.20	1.00
Ribbon	n/a							
Label	1	0.05	0.05	label supplier	00034	0.50	1.00	5.00
MATERIAL 1M=								
Front: Red Stripe Jersey	8	7.00	0.88	fabric supplier	red 332	8.75	17.50	87.50
Back: Black mesh	7	4.50	0.64	fabric supplier	black 001	6.43	12.86	64.29
Gusset: self - red stripe	25	7.00	0.28	fabric supplier	red 332	2.80	5.60	28.00
TOTAL			1.96			19.58	39.16	195.79
MANUFACTURING			4.50			45.00	90.00	450.00
TOTAL			6.46			64.58	129.16	645.79

PATTERN NUMBER:

NAME & SIGNATURE:

The cost sheet should have all the information you need to re-make the same piece again. You should include the description, colours, your supplier, and your supplier code.

1. In the total column, you need to multiply (x) the cost and the amount. The cost is per metre; the amount is gained by measuring the finished garment. So 1.8m came from measuring both legs and the waist as the same elastic was being used. In the total column is the amount it costs for one garment.

2. Enter your supplier and the code they use so you have all the information in one place, if you need to re-order anything.

3. I always like to work out how much it would cost for 10, 20 and 100 pieces, because often you're dealing with minimums and it also gets you thinking on a bigger scale.

4. Do the same for any trims you are adding.

5. For materials, the amount is how much one metre of fabric will make of one piece. For example you can get 8 fronts out of one metre of re stripey fabric.

6. For the total you divide the cost by the amount. Each front will cost you £0.88

7. Do the same for the back and gusset.

8. Add all the totals up. This will represent how much it takes in materials alone to make one piece.

9. Next add in your manufacturing cost this you get from your manufacturer.

(The extras would be things like handling costs, threads, or any trims that are hard to calculate)

Blank Costing Sheet: Free permission to use is given

COMPANY: | **STYLE NAME/NUMBER:**

GARMENT DESCRIPTION:

COMPONENT	AMOUNT (M)	COST (£)	TOTAL (£)	SUPPLIER	CODE	10 UNITS	20 UNITS	100 UNITS
TRIMS								
MATERIAL								
Front:								
TOTAL =								
TOTAL								
MANUFACTURING								
TOTAL								

PATTERN NUMBER:

NAME & SIGNATURE:

Sheet1

Mark up

Once you understand the basic rules of costing – be sure to add in the indirect costs before moving on to the mark up.

Basically

Costs of fabric + trims + labour + business overheads + profit = Garment cost

After you deduct all of the expenses (the direct expenses and the indirect expenses) from the revenue you generate from the lingerie you sell. You are left with the profit.

For smaller companies the margin and mark up will be higher than the bigger mass-producing companies due to the volume they manufacture. Your lingerie may also be subjective to what the market will bear – i.e. it depends on where you want to position yourself in the market.

Tip: **The bigger companies will always be able to compete on price, have something else to offer.**

Knowing what level to price your lingerie is always a tricky one. There is rule of thumb for mark ups. I would take into consideration the following as a guide for your price point.

1. Your costs (direct and indirect)
2. Hurdle rate (how much profit you need to make)
3. What your competitors are charging (your positioning)
4. What the customer is willing to pay (the benefit that you are providing).

Shops or boutiques will roughly add a 2.3% - 3.5% mark up depending on the type of shop. Some will go even higher. Bear that in mind when you approach the buyers (i.e. selling your lingerie for £10 to a buyer they will mark it up to sell at £23-£35). If the shop wants your lingerie at a lower cost than you can afford either walk away; or if you think it will gain you great exposure consider doing a tiny run and absorb the costs elsewhere – however, remember if your label isn't making a profit then you have no label.

Chapter Thirteen

Manufacturing

The decline of manufacturing

Manufacturing generally in the UK & USA has declined rapidly in the past years, lingerie manufacturing even more so. In the 90's there were three lingerie manufacturers alone in the Lincolnshire area (UK). Now there are only a couple of manufactures in the whole of the UK designated to the production of bras and briefs.

Manufacturing Overseas

The main reason for off shore manufacturing is to reduce production costs. However, this will incur expenses such as shipping, inventory, time spent communicating, import/export restrictions, and other costs which may occur. Also the minimums will be higher.

Handmade Lingerie V's Factory manufacturing

Depending on your label and the quantity that you produce, will determine whether or not you hand make the lingerie yourself or outsource it to a manufacturer. Each decision has pros and cons.

Making the lingerie yourself allows you to do smaller runs of each line, however don't underestimate the amount of time it will take you, is your time better spent doing other things? Only you know which method is correct for you. If you do decide on outsourcing I would recommend that you have an idea how lingerie is assembled as this will save you money and less confusion in the future, especially if you are dealing with off shore manufacturers.

Contact details of UK Manufacturers

THE FACTORY
UNIT 14
167 CRUSADER ESTATE
HERMITAGE ROAD
LONDON
N4 1LZ

0044 (0) 208 800 9979
thefactory@fashion-enter.com

www.fashioncapital.com

AJM SEWING
THE WORKS
MORGAN STREET
NEW TRADEGAR
NP24 6AE
WALES
UK

0044 (0) 1443 820 969
enquiries@ajmsewing.co.uk

www.ajmsewing.co.uk

Permission has been
granted form all
manufacturers to
publish their details

'The Factory' manufacturers soft separates not underwire bras. It also runs a stitching academy, which is collaborated with ASOS.

Contact details of a
UK Lingerie Sample Making Unit

Maxine's Lingerie Creatives is a lingerie sample-making unit specialising in designing and creating intimate apparel, and clothing for small to medium sized companies or individuals. For those who feel they aren't ready to go straight to a manufacturer and need help with initial patterns, sample or grading then contact.

Website: www.lingeriesamplemaker.co.uk
Email: enquiries@lingeriesamplemaker.co.uk

Chapter Fourteen

Studio vs Location

When reaching the photo shoot stage you should now understand and have a strong identity of your brand. This will enable you to choose where you want your fashion shoot to take place.

Getting the location right is important especially if you want to convey a narrative within your shot. When done successfully this can strengthen your brand as it embodies the whole fashion atmosphere of the moment.

Studio shots are great if you want to control the lighting and stabilize conditions. Usually the shoot is much quicker than if you on location somewhere.

When starting out if money is tight, you can offer a TFP situation (time for prints). Some models and make up artists work TFCD, (time for CD) which means that they have the photos on a CD to print when they want. While it is cheaper to produce a CD rather than the prints bear in mind if you give out a CD you are giving permission for your images to be reproduced at the models or artists discretion. Another alternative is to pay the model with the lingerie that they're modeling.

Video of the photo shoot

Another good way, to not only gain exposure but also allow buyers to see the lingerie on is to do a video of the photo shoot.

I did a very basic one back in 2009 – http://www.youtube.com/watch?v=VSlql3u2wgA

I got my inspiration from Ophelia Fancy – http://www.youtube.com/watch?v=MR46F9hD-6w

Typical equipment needed

DSLR Camera - Not necessarily top of the range but decent

Flash Guns - To show the garments in the best possible light

Light Meter - Makes camera setup quicker and more efficient

Light box - For still life and flat shots

Compact camera - Easy to document certain features setups quickly

Backgrounds and Backdrops - These can also look fun used outside.

Tripod - Keep those images still when needed.

Laptop - For photo summarising and editing

Chapter Fifteen

additional items
TO CONSIDER

Website

A modern well presented website is now expected for most businesses or fashion labels, with the convenience of people reading about your label in their own time. Having web presence expands your market significantly. It's recommended to get a website as soon as possible even if you only have a holding page with how to contact you. Plus it makes it easier for buyers or press to look you up. If you're paying for a website be sure that you can change the content of the pages and there isn't a hidden cost for changes at a later date.

Labels

You must have care labels and swing tickets on your lingerie these are needed on your labels, and it should read:

1. How to wash the garment
2. Where the garment was made
3. The fabric content
4. The size

Some brands have all their information on one label; others like to have their brand label, then another label with all the information. When starting out it's quite acceptable to have the fabric content on the swing ticket rather than printed on a label that is inserted into the garment.

If your website is the same name as your label name be savvy and get your garment label printed up with the web address.

Business Stationary

Business cards are an inexpensive yet indispensable way to introduce yourself and your label. Include your phone number and email address because people always prefer one way to contact you to the other.

Since your business card often makes that all-important first impression you want to stand out from the pack and give yourself an edge. Relate the card to your style of your label. If you design very delicate lingerie, you don't want a really heavy print or a dark business card.

Have your cards printed on good heavy weight card if your card feels flimsy it'll leave the impression with people that they are dealing with a small company and that you're not really serious about it.

Remember, your goal isn't to produce a work of art; it's to produce a business card that clearly communicates what you do and how to reach you. If recipients can't read the contact information you'll lose sales.

With regards to headed paper make sure your logo can be converted to black and white easily. Then you can put the logo and information on anything you need to print out and send. This then won't cost you a fortune using a coloured logo the whole time.

There are hundreds of places to get your business cards produced
www.cardsmadeeasy.com - www.betterprint.co.uk - www.**typoretum**.com
www.vistaprint.com - www.goodprint.co.uk - www.moo.com

Chapter Sixteen

Buyers, Trade Shows & SELLING YOUR PRODUCT

Contacting Lingerie Designers

The best way is simply the old fashioned way. Once you have your design (and cost sorted). Find departments or boutiques (in some boutiques it's often the owner) that sell lingerie in which you think your lingerie brand will sit along side, in terms of style and price. Call them to make an appointment and follow each phone call up with an email. Include either a link to your website or jpegs of your work so they have a reminder of who you are.

When meeting with the buyer don't promise more than you can realistically deliver. This includes quantity and lead times (the amount of time it will take you to deliver the lingerie). Most boutiques only pay after the lingerie has been delivered, some insist on 30 days after it's been delivered. If it's a new boutique opening insist on a percentage being paid up front. You don't want to be totally out of pocket especially if you're working a season or two ahead.

Create a purchase order which lists the details of the agreement, date of order, date of delivery, exactly what they have ordered, and get them to sign this. Also have a terms and conditions policy to give to the buyer. This usually contains information on delivery costs if they cancel the order, and payment details.

* If you are unsure of the layout of your purchase order – Microsoft Office has free downloads in either Microsoft Word or Microsoft Excel. *www.office.microsoft.com* Once there, either look in the templates section or search for 'purchase order'. They have over 1000 different free download templates.

The importance of a newsletter

With a website you only have one chance to turn a customer into a buyer before they leave. Having made all these contacts to buyers it's vital that you keep them informed of what your label is up to. This will make it easier when you contact them back again with your next season's lingerie designs. Your mailing list will become your most important asset in the long run. I would also put a newsletter out once a month so the buyer doesn't forget you. Keep it brief, and to the point, you don't want to bury your message by waffling on. It also gives the buyer the chance to get to know more about your label.

The Pros & Cons with Sale or Return!

If you're heading down the SoR (Sale or Return) route make sure you and the retailer have a receipt of the lingerie you have delivered. Decide before hand if you set the RRP (Recommended Retail Price), or if they do. As well as giving a receipt also get the buyer to sign your terms of agreement, on this should be:

1. How long the items are to stay in the shop – a season?
2. When you re-stock items – do you restock continuously so that they always have a full size range?
3. How they will pay you at the end of the month?
4. When will you finally take the items back?

If your work is a huge success enquire about changing from SoR to them buying wholesale. Be prepared for returns being damaged – include this in your terms and conditions that the shop is held responsible for any damages.

Showing at a Trade Show

Never book a table or space at a trade show that you've never attended. All the information from trade show organizers about foot traffic, buyer attendance, and press coverage will never provide the same insight that walking around the actual trade show will.

Contact the organizers of the event to clarify what visitors the show attracts; and your exact layout of the area you will be paying for. Usually you can buy a booth package with the walls already in place or a raw package. The raw package is for labels that have custom built booths. Most small labels go for booth packages; I would recommend covering the walls with drapes or fabrics. Also find out the finer details, size of the table, whether you can attach anything to walls, if there will be an electrical outlet available and anything else that may or may not be included.

Have a portfolio of your work available as part of the display. To get the most out of the trade show, send out mailings to buyers inviting them to come and stop by, set up appointments if you can as well. Take notes of who people are, when they hand you their business card. Most importantly follow up with everyone who handed you his or her business card – straight away – when you get back to your studio (or kitchen table).

List of Trade shows

FRANCE
- Lyon Mode City (www.lyonmodecity.com)
  Running for the past 30 years; exhibiting lingerie and swimwear.
- Salon International de la Lingerie (www.lingerie-paris.com)
  Comprising of exhibitors, future trends and catwalk shows.

GERMANY
- Dessous Messe Wallau (www.dessous.muveo.de)
  National and International showcase new collections in lingerie,
  day and nightwear, beach and swimwear and menswear.

UK
- The Lingerie Collective (www.thelingeriecollective.com)
  Supports independent UK & International fashion lingerie brands
- Moda Lingerie and Swimwear (www.moda-uk.co.uk)
  Editorially-led catwalk shows, seminars and lingerie and swimwear
  exhibitors.

USA
- Curve NY (www.curvexpo.com)
  Exhibiting high-end brands in lingerie, swimwear, and menswear.
- The International Lingerie Show (www.lingerieshow.cc/)
  This show leans towards the adult theme of lingerie.
  Under 18's not allowed.
- Miami Lingerie and Swimshow (www.swimshow.com)
  A well known Swimwear show has now introduced the
  showing of lingerie.

WORLDWIDE
- Interfiliere
  The Lingerie trade show has international events in Paris,
  New York, Shanghai, Hong Kong and Las Vegas.

Chapter Seventeen

RELEASES
Creating a Press Release

A press release is an official statement issued to the media, which entices them to report your news to the public. It's traditionally written in the third person, a good press release will be the difference between free publicity and no publicity. Press releases are often sent alone or part of a full press kit, which may be accompanied by a pitch letter. Remember as your label grows and changes, so should your press release. Don't keep sending out the same press release a year down the line.

Formatting a Press Release

Your Press release should:

- Be about 500 words long.
- Double spaced
- Include the date of the release, eg 'For immediate release (date)' or Embargoed for (time/date)
- Headline written in bold – choose a headline that makes the reader want to read more.
- Paragraph 1: Summarise your story - who, what, where, when & why.
- Paragraph 2: Go into more detail that you have outlined in the first paragraph.
- Paragraph 3. "Quotes from you or someone relevant to the story" if there are quotes.
- Paragraph 4. Extra relevant information.
- Put your website at the end.
- Type END or ###
- Use your headline as the subject in your email not 'press release'

Provide background information in case they run a longer story, outline what you have to offer, ie pictures, interviews etc.

Sample of Press Release (Circa 2005) is over the page

This was my very first press release , it was sent out before the launch of my website.

THE LAUNCH OF NEW ERA IN LINGERIE!

Lingerie, but not as we know it...announcing the launch of Vanjo, an eco-friendly brand, specifically tailored for busty ladies with small backs. Vanjo was born out of frustration of one woman - Laurie van Jonsson – trying to find a bra that fitted, without compromising on style.

Laurie, a 30DD herself, is a fashion graduate of De Montfort University with a specialism in contour and lingerie, putting her in the prime position to work out a solution. She spent three years designing lingerie and swimwear for top high street stores like Next, River Island and Topshop, then launched her own branded swimwear in Thailand in European sizes, and travelled round the world and continued selling her own brand of swimwear, to a wider audience. Now she's back in the UK with Vanjo – a fusion of style, fit and comfort to rescue beleaguered big-boobed ladies everywhere.

The inspiration behind Vanjo comes from a desire for women to embrace their curves and enjoy wearing fabulous underwear in a design they love that actually fits properly, rather than having to choose between fashion and fit.

Increasing awareness in the marketplace of the importance of well-fitting lingerie has meant that many token efforts have been made by larger purveyors of underwear to provide larger sizes. However, many of the larger sizes only pay lip service to the problem – a larger size doesn't necessarily mean a good fit. What's more, the environmental ethos of Vanjo – which ranges from a 28" to a 36" and from a C to a FF cup – has meant that small ranges are available using stock fabrics and trims, creating less wastage – a huge improvement on the large scale fabric waste that is standard practise in the rag trade.

A selection of the Vanjo product range is already being stocked in the Oxford Street Branch of Topshop, as well as in smaller boutiques around the UK. The Vanjo site – www.vanjo.co.uk will be up and running in March. The designs mix flirty romance and a retro feel; funky dressed up style and classic chic. The results are inspired by vintage prints and delicate trims, with an individuality that shines through – girls just wanna have fun!

~ END ~

Working with a Journalist

1. A follow on call can help develop your press release; though if you really want to get your post printed call first to pitch your story and then follow up with your release.

2. Plan your calls most papers are morning editions, this means that journalists' deadlines range from 2pm local time don't call that time. It's best to call 10am to noon local time.

3. Remember the editor isn't interested in helping you make money or driving visitors to your site. They are just looking for a story that will be interesting to their readers.

4. Don't be put off, there might be a whole host of reasons that your story didn't get used. A bigger story may have just pushed it out.

Chapter Eighteen

COURSES

Furthering your knowledge.

For those who are interested in wanting to attend courses either
full time/part time or simply just for a weekend there are plenty
of courses which can be found at www.emagister.com. Emagister
is an international website, pick your flag representing your country
which will lead you to your country's homepage, then simply type
in 'Lingerie courses' for a courses near you.

Birmingham - Day and Evening
http://www.birminghamschoolofsewing.co.uk

Hertfordshire - Day course
http://www.rebeccawoollard.co.uk

Kensington & Chelsea College   -   Evening and Day classes
http://www.kcc.ac.uk

Leeds & Ipswich - Day classes
http://www.thesewingsessions.co.uk

Leicestershire - Day courses
http://www.schoolofsewing.co.uk

Demontfort (University Leicester) - BA Hons (3 yrs) & Short
http://www.dmu.ac.uk/home.aspx

London - Photography Day classes
http://www.studiotimephoto.com photography

London - Evening or Weekend classes
http://lingeriemasterclasses.blogspot.co.uk

London college of Fashion - BA Hons (3 yrs) & Short
http://www.fashion.arts.ac.uk

London - Photography Course
http://focushubcourses.com

London - Short courses
http://www.prescottandmackay.co.uk

London - Short courses
http://www.lingeriesamplemaker.co.uk

Morley college - Weekend and Day courses
http://www.morleycollege.ac.uk

Central Nottingham College - Day course
http://www.centralnottingham.ac.uk

Sheffield - Day courses
http://www.englishcouture.co.uk

Southampton - Day course
http://www.barryrogersschoolofsewing.co.uk

Truro - Short course
http://www.barryrogersschoolofsewing.co.uk

WORDS

How to become a Lingerie Designer was first launched as an e-book along with the website www.howtobeomealingeriedesigner.com A contact page can be found if you have any further questions. I will answer as best I can and if I don't have the answers I will point you in the right direction where that answer can be found. Also on the website is a blog you can follow.
I hope your love for lingerie leads you to fulfilling your desire to launch you own lingerie label. If that is the route you choose then let me know as even though I continue to design, I'm still in awe of seeing other people's work and success.

If you're still unsure where to go from here? On the following pages are interviews from a few lingerie designers. All who have started their lingerie label within the last eight years. They are in order of how many years they have been trading. Each mini interview ends with the question.

"What words of advice would you give aspiring designers?"

Personally, the best advice I ever got given was:

"If you want to do something, just start, don't wait until you're 100% ready, the moment will have passed; just start."

Interviews with
LINGERIE DESIGNERS

LORNA DREW of
"LORNA DREW"
www.lornadrew.com

What year did you start Lorna Drew? January 2012

Can you give a brief description of the style of Lorna Drew? Chic,
Elegant,
Innovative
and very British.

Did you have any formal lingerie design (brief history of how you came to design)?

I went to De Montfort Uni and did the Contour degree, I did 3 work placements whilst at Uni for small and big brands, and I got my first Job after winning a lingerie design competition. My graduating collection was chosen by 'Lingerie Buyer' magazine as the graduate collection of the year in 2006, and 'WGSN' announced me as a young designer to watch on as part of "Their Generation Now" article.

What makes something worth making?

For me Lingerie is very emotional; the garments have to improve the quality of women's lives in some way.
My brand is Nursing lingerie, so my garments are designed to offer the full package, ultimate comfort, adjustable support, workable solutions and an elegant design. For me lingerie is worth making if it makes women feel good in some way. When I get letters and emails from Woman writing to tell me how much they love our bras, that's when I know all the hard work is worth it.

What is your ideal day?

My Ideal day would be when I finally get everything done on my "To do list." Which very rarely happens as I always underestimate how long it takes to get things done. Or winning that allusive high profile big customer, for me that's always a massive thrill.

What does the future hold?

If I had a crystal ball I would tell you! I hope that the business grows, we have just started working with your retailers in the USA and Europe so the brand is growing internationally, which is fantastic for us, it's just a case of keeping all the momentum going.

Who inspires you?

Real Women inspire me most from all walks of life, when I design something I always have a customer in mind with a personality and that's why I name the ranges a woman's name, that way it gives ranges real personality.

I'm most inspired by courageous women with a voice, women that speak out about their views and encourage others, whether intentionally or not. These women inspire me to evolve in designing for women.

Some of the most inspirational women to me are My Mother, Anita Roddick, Emma Wimhurst, Vivian Westwood, Amy Winehouse, Hollie McNash, Michelle Mone, Wangari Maathai, Tracey Emin, Amy Owen-Drew, Zandra Rhodes, Natasha Walter, Margate Thatcher, Lady Gaga , my old A-Level art teacher Mrs Jolly and the Queen.

What words of advice would give aspiring designers?

My top tip is DO YOUR HOMEWORK BEFORE YOU START ANYTHING!

Research your market and do a business plan, you need to make sure you have a unique product or brand and the customers' needs will be met buy your Brand before you start any of the fun and creative work.

It sounds boring but a well thought out business plan with clear goals makes it easier to see how the brand will develop and allows you to measure your success.

Lorna Drew

FRAUKE NAGEL of "FRAULEIN ANNIE"
www.frauleinannie.com

What year did you start Fräulein Annie?

I started working on the brand in early 2010 and launched the first collection in September 2011.

Can you give a brief description of Fräulein Annie?

Fräulein Annie makes high quality lingerie and swimwear that is beautiful and glamorous as well as supportive and body flattering. It shall enhance the body's appearance and boost women's confidence.

Do you have formal lingerie design (brief history of how you came to design)?

From the age of 6, textiles and being creative are my major interests and skills in life. I studied textile design and started my career as a knitwear designer. Lingerie is essentially made of knitted fabrics and this is how I got into it over the years.

Do you prefer sketching designs or actually constructing them?

Both. I'd be bored if I'd have to do only one or the other.

What is key to good design? A design is made of different elements that fit together like a jigsaw. Good design is meaningful and of purpose, there can be an awful lot of thought that goes into it to make it work. I like to inject feeling and a certain mood into my designs, each one of them is telling a story.

Three things you love about your studio? I love the airiness and the light, the view out of the large windows. My pieces of vintage furniture that I collected over the years.

Has your lingerie label taken you where you thought it would? It has sent me on an exciting and challenging journey on which I meet a lot of interesting and lovely people. I couldn't have predicted it, it's rewarding on an emotional level.

What words of advice would you give aspiring designers? Do your research, find you niche, focus! Listen to your customers but stay true to yourself at the same time. Keep your overheads tight, only spend money when it's absolutely necessary and as little as possible.

Frauke Nagel

KRISS SOONIK *of* "KRISS SOONIK"

www.kriss-soonik.com

What year did you start Kriss Soonik?

Kriss Soonik started in January 2009

Can you give a brief description of the style of Kriss Soonik?

Kriss Soonik gives the "underwear as outerwear" concept a fresh and fun twist.

Did you have any formal lingerie design (brief history of how you came to design)?

No.

Before I properly started my label I had been designing for five years as a hobby. Always on the side of either working (Agent Provocateur, Madame V) or studying (BA in Estonian Business School; MA at the London College of Fashion, Strategic Fashion Marketing). I had always known I want to do my own thing but lingerie found me.

What is the key to good design?	Comfort and fit, and the design itself.
What motivates you?	Progress. And the ability to do something I love and make people smile with it.
What three things define beauty in a woman?	I would go with one – personality.
What are your top goals in your brand?	The world is our playground. We just have to grab every opportunity we have to spread our wings in the global market.
What words of advice would you give inspiring designers?	Go for it but be prepared to work not only hard but smart. If you are passionate and love what you do, you´ll get far.

*Image by Anu Hammer

Kriss Soonik

MARNI FRANKS *of*
"THOUSAND DANCERS"

www.thousanddancers.com.au

When did you start Thousand Dancers? 2009

Can you give a brief description of the style of Thousand Dancers? The range is designed for the Australian climate concentrating on natural fibers like silk and cotton printed in Australia. The range uses vintage-inspired cuts that are given a playful updating with pretty prints. All our prints are designed by handcrafted methods in house and exclusive to Thousand Dancers

Did you have any formal lingerie design (brief history of how you came to design)? I have no formal lingerie or fashion design training; instead I studied prints and graphics and learnt my fashion knowledge through my work. I have a bachelor in graphic design and a masters in textile design. I began my design life as a graphic designer in Brisbane before my obsession with lingerie and textiles saw me relocate to Melbourne to design for boutique lingerie label, Sabi Lingerie followed, by a second relocation to Sydney to design for underwear giant Bonds Underwear, Pacific Brands.

Who is your favourite designer (doesn't have to be Lingerie)?	My favourite lingerie designers are Princesse-Tam Tam and Guia la Bruna, I love their natural fibers and obsession with prints. However, print-wise, my two favorites are Eley Kishimoto and Mina Perhonen.
Has your lingerie label taken you where you thought it would?	I had hoped the label would involve more international travel, however, I've had some gorgeous interstate sales trips where I've met some beautiful storeowners and suppliers.
Three things you love about the location of your studio?	My studio is now in the front room of my house. My house is a sweet workers cottage in inner-city Brisbane, that is so very quiet, but close to everything you could need. I love that I have everything I need right there with me.
What motivates you?	I'm motivated mostly by the amazing fashion designers Australia has like Romance was Born; Therese Rawsthorne; Rebecca Manning or Antipodium.
What words of advice would you have for aspiring designers?	The most individual thing about your designs is you. Make sure you reference your self, your heritage and your loves in what you do.

Marni Franks

ANDREA BILLARD *of*
"ANDREA BILLLARD"

www.andreabillard.com

*Can you give a brief
description of the style
of Andrea Billard?*
Andrea Billard | Haute Lingerie is an independent luxury
lingerie brand based in England. Launched in 2009 by
Creative Director Andrea Billard, it has attracted exten-
sive media interest in the UK, US, Middle East, South
America and Europe. The fit and style of the AB-HL
collections are designed to compliment your wardrobe
and lifestyle, and to enhance your feeling of confidence
and glamour. The brand is designed, sourced and made in
England, mixing strong femininity with subtle sexuality,
appealing to those with a love of luxury and innovative
designs.

Andrea Billard is part of a new wave of British design
talent. Her mission is to create beautiful, modern lingerie,
which has a sensual feel and brings out the beauty and
power in every woman. In a short period of time, Andrea
has built a reputation of exceptional quality, strong design

signature and is passionate about promoting UK skills and craftsmanship. As Creative Director and owner of the company, she oversees all aspects of the business and as well as being a very hands-on designer and continues to steer the company forward to find new and exciting ways to develop the brand both nationally and internationally. "80% of my collections are sold to women. It's never been about selling lingerie for the benefit and pleasure of men. It's a brand created by a woman for other women and it's the woman's pleasure that is paramount. " – Andrea Billard

Did you have any formal lingerie design (brief history of how you came to design?)?

No I was trained in general fashion but specialized in sportswear (golf and equestrian and the football kits and sports merchandise) when I left college. When I decided I wanted to work for myself, lingerie was the only thing I hadn't actually design and as I fancied a challenge, I studied the market for 12 months, learned as much as I could about the construction of a bra etc.

What are you hoping for the future?

I have recently signed with a US distributor so I am looking forward to working in the US market as well as expanding in the UK.

What three things are hard about being a Lingerie designer?

It's a very expensive business to set up. Getting people to have faith in a new brand. Finding continuing funding to keep it going.

Do you listen to music at all whilst designing?

Yes - Aha (I'm an 80's fan!) and classical music which I find relaxing. I don't like too much modern music.

What do you enjoy most about your work process? Seeing the product go from idea, to sketch to sample and then seeing it called in by stylists for a celebrity or photo shoot.

What advice do you have for aspiring designers? Make sure you study the market first, know your price point. Think how you will market the product so that it stands out amongst your competitors. Make sure you have sufficient funding in place and keep an eye on spending. Be aware that very few brands are 'overnight successes' - you have to be in it for the long haul.

Andrea Billard

VICTORIA HOLT *of*
"FRED AND GINGER"
www.fredandginger.com

What year did your start Fred and Ginger?

September 2007

Can you give a brief description of Fred and Ginger?

Fred & Ginger is a high-end luxury label, specialising in lingerie, designed in London and all produced by wonderfully talented ladies in the UK.

Do you have formal lingerie design (brief history of how you came to design)?

I do not have a lingerie background but believed that I could take a different slant on the industry and stand out from the crowd. I graduated with a BA (hons) in Fashion and Textiles in 2000 and immediately took up my position with Jenny Packham. Learning all areas of the business from sales and marketing to PR and Design. I eventually gained position as head designer for Jenny Packham Bride whilst simultaneously working as senior designer for the mainline and catwalk pieces. I left Jenny Packham in 2005 to take a year out to travel the world solo. I returned with a brand name and passion to start my own luxury lingerie label Fred & Ginger, bringing with me a wealth of business knowledge and experience in the luxury industry.

What three things have inspired you lately? Beautiful comments from consumers of Fred & Ginger, discovering I'm pregnant, the new Great Gatsby film.

What motivates you? A passion for my business, a need for success, my husband and family.

Has your lingerie label taken you where you thought it would? No not quite.. I am still waiting for my big break!

What three things define beauty to you in a woman? Confidence, a nice smile and a positive attitude.

What words of advice would you give aspiring designers? You need a lot of grit and determination. Don't celebrate too much when things are going great and don't get too upset when the chips are down. It's a roller coaster ride but if you keep a level head you should be emotionally stable which is what you need to run the business!

Victoria Holt

CLAIRE BRADBURY *of*
"IRRESISTIBLE LINGERIE"

www.irresistible-lingerie.com

What year did you start Irresistible Lingerie?

I set the company up in October 2006 and spent the next 10 months designing and manufacturing the first collection. We had a launch party in Manchester city centre in July 2007.

Can you give a brief description of the style of Irresistible Lingerie?

Our style has evolved over the past 5 years and changed as we have grown as a brand. Our luxury collection combines unexpected colour combinations, with exquisite details and prints to create a sophisticated and beautiful collection.

Did you have any formal lingerie design (brief history of how you came to design)?

I studied Art and Design at college and then completed a BA (Hons) Fashion Design with Technology degree at Manchester Metropolitan University. I had developed a passion for lingerie design so went to De Montfort University to take some of their short courses in Bra fitting and Bra making.

What do you love about your work? I love creating and developing a collection from an idea in my head right through to the finished garment and I love meeting customers and buyers. It's a great feeling when someone tries one of my products on and it fits them perfectly or they email me and tell me how happy they are with their purchase. I have had some great feedback from customers.

What three things have inspired you lately? I am always inspired by colours, so it can be the sky on a drive home, or the colour combinations on a magazine cover. Life inspires me.

What is your dream? To continue to enjoy creating beautiful lingerie and selling to customers and boutiques worldwide.

How do you keep your studio organized? My design area is creative chaos! but I keep the packing area and my stock rail tidy and organized and I have many filing cabinets and cupboards. I use Omni Focus which is a software program for Apple Mac's to keep on top of my to do list.

What words of advice would you give aspiring designers? From a practical point of view, learn everything you can about the industry, visit trade shows, talk to designers and do as many work placements as possible.

From a personal point of view, do what you love, dare to dream, and follow your heart.

Claire Bradbury

CATHERINE CLAVERING *of*
"KISS ME DEADLY"

www.kissmedeadly.co.uk

What year did you start Kiss Me Deadly?	We started trading in 2006, very part time, it didn't really turn into anything until 2007.
Can you give a brief description of the style of Kiss Me Deadly?	Vintage inspired lingerie sets, without the retro kitsch.
Did you have any formal lingerie design (brief history of how you came to design)?	Not a bean! I do sketches (I have an art GCSE if that helps?) and some other poor sod has to work out how to make it work technically. Mind you, I've discovered that that's the level many fashion degrees bring you out at, so I don't worry about it too much. I do know far more about hosiery than most people though, which is indirectly how I ended up doing this, as I was involved in a hosiery retail outlet online. We'd all agreed there was a market for lingerie to go with vintage style stockings, but I had the most almighty row with my then business

partner when he scrapped the plans for it - after I'd sorted it all out from scratch and the samples had arrived, and the week before my MSc research was due in. After considerable cursing, I wrote 10,000 words on a Foucouldian discourse analysis of constructions of the vulva, illustrated with a classic painting of a female nude (allegedly to illustrate a crucial point about the inter-relationship of taboo and power, but actually just to see if I could annoy my lecturers).

Frankly, after doing that, it seemed like all the hard work was over and it would be as simple to just carry on with the lingerie brand on my own. At the time I thought it would be a useful counterpoint to a career in mental health; by the end of the post-grad I was too disabled by M.E to carry on with it, so now I have full time knickers!

What makes something worth making? It has to be either reasonably likely to be profitable or something that will make a buzz (some things don't sell that well but bring people to look at you). Sorry, we're not at the stage where I can make things just for fun yet.

What drives you? I really don't want to have to deal with ATOS.

What three things have inspired you lately? We're planning our AW12 shoots; we're doing f'*ked up fairytales, so our fans have been telling us which characters they love. This means I am currently inspired by axes, witches, spangly horned headdresses and tiaras.

What do you love about your studio? I don't have one. I have a front room with some stuff in it and two cats who get in the way instead. I'm actually quite fond of the cats, but don't let them know!

Get your head round marketing, social media, and sums and statistics. It doesn't matter how great your product is if you haven't got that together or find someone who can do it for you.

Brand identity is not actually just marketing people's bullshit, it really does make a difference, Yes, it was a shock to me too.

Catherine Clavering

AYTEN ROBERTS *of*
"AYTEN GASSON"

www.aytengasson.com

What year did you start
Ayten Gasson?

I launched the label in 2005 and specialise in silk lingerie trimmed with vintage lace.

Can you give a brief
description of the style
of Ayten Gasson?

We are a UK based lingerie company with a firm commitment to producing in the UK and an eye to ethical and sustainable sources. Items will be designed, sourced and manufactured in the UK as much as possible. Our style is sophisticated glamour, with inspiration being drawn from stunning styles of the 1920s-1940s. Designs are also inspired by vintage lingerie shapes and styles.

Did you have any
formal lingerie
design (brief history
of how you came to
design)?

I have actually had no lingerie training but I come from a long line of designers and makers, as have always been around people in the industry. Not a very academic family! We include a bridal wear designer, a rug designer (if that's the correct term), a sample machinist, an overlocker in a London production unit, and a tailor.

I knew from a young age that I had an interest in the fashion industry. I understood that only 20% of your time is actually spent sitting down designing, while the rest of the time is spent sampling, making, planning, and lots of paperwork! Here's a brief outline of my design background:

- BTEC National Diploma - *London College of Fashion*
  1997 – 1998
- BA (HONS) Fashion Print - *Central Saint Martins*
  1998 – 2002
- Work Placement - *Keeler Gordon Textile Design* [Co]
  London - April 2000 – July 2000
- 1 Year Work Placement - *Eley Kishimoto*
  London August 2000 – July 2001

Three things you love about the location of your studio?

I am currently in the process of moving out of my North London studio and relocating the business to Brighton. I lived in Brighton for 6 years and the business was first set up in the living room of my one bedroom flat. I love the creativity of Brighton and feel it is filled with opportunities. The architecture is also inspiring while the University constantly provides the city with a motivated new group of creative people.

What is your ideal day?

I love the days I get to spend designing and sampling. Unfortunately when you have your own business these days are few and far between. I love it when I return from a visit to Nottingham with a bag full of lace samples and trims and can sit in the studio and have a play. I tend to prefer making up samples than sitting with a paper and drawing my designs.

Why did you start Ayten Gasson? Upon graduating from university I was disheartened to find many of the UK based manufactures and design houses had closed as designers now searched for a cheaper alternative overseas. I grew up in Archway, N London, and the six garment factories behind my family's house had closed by the time I finished my studies, with a lot of them now turning into flats. I started to look for design work, either in print or in fashion, but a large number of design jobs had moved to Europe, mainly in Paris or Bologna. I was actively looking for a design job for over two years while working in gift shops and on the high street. I was told about The Princes' Trusts Enterprise Programme, and through them I managed to secure funding to launch my own label. I decided that I wanted to promote the UK fashion industry and highlight the traditional skills, which the UK was once celebrated for.

Has you Lingerie label taken you where you thought it would? I thought that after 6 years I would be making more money. No matter how much money you make you will spend as much trying to make it. Though it is rewarding when you see your achievements in the press or in boutiques. The continued decline in the UK manufacturing industry has changed the path I wanted the business to take. I would love to say I would only use English lace but with the news of one of my suppliers closing soon I am worried that I might one day run out of options!

What words of advice would you give aspiring designers? One of the greatest challenges is trying to make the brand stand out from all the other new and old brands in the UK. Everyone has a specific USP but its hard work trying to get yours noticed. We are a small brand, so it's hard to compete with a larger brand who has someone specifically working on PR.

contd... The best reward is when you get positive feedback from a customer. I try and answer all our customer comments and requests myself and it is lovely to hear why they have bought a specific piece. We have also had a fantastic response on our new eco range, which highlighted the gap in the market and lets me know I am listening to the people who buy and wear my lingerie.

Ayten Roberts

IGOR PACEMSKI *of*
"YES MASTER"

www.yes-master.com

What year did you start Yes Master?

2005.

Can you give a brief description of the style of Yes Master?

Sophisticated, modern, high end, intelligent & wearable.

Did you have any formal lingerie design (brief history of how you came to design)?

Nope! UCL quantum chemistry, an MSc in polymer science, currently doing an MBA at Warwick.

Who is your favourite designer (doesn't have to be lingerie)?

Galiano, early Gaultier, McQueen under Lee (sorry Sarah), La Perla Black when it was good.

What three things surprise you about being a lingerie designer?

Nothing ever surprises me. I came into the industry after having had very big jobs, so I sort of took it in my stride (annoyingly).

What three things define beauty to you in a woman? Brains, natural elegance, come to bed eyes.

What is your favourite part of the day? Midnight or dusk...

What words of advice would you give aspiring designers? Imagine been poor, tired, hungry, downtrodden, down in the dumps and multiply in tenfold and that what awaits you for the first 2-3 years. On the plus side, if you survive that, great things await x

Igor Pacemski

CHLOE HAMBLEN *of*
"LASCIVIOUS"
www.lascivious.co.uk

What year did your start Lascivious? The brand was founded and launched late in 2004.

Can you give a brief description of Lascivious? Lascivious: las·civ·i·ous (luh-siv-ee-uhs)
Adjective: Given to or expressing lust; lecherous. Exciting sexual desires; salacious.

Lascivious has been fuelled by a passion for the aesthetics of sex, and sophisticated, modern design. It is an indulgent and directional lingerie brand, with a growing list of celebrity fans and accolades from every major fashion publication. Lascivious inspires those searching for unique, fashion-forward lingerie with which to empower and seduce. Collections include seasonal fashion ranges, best-selling Classics, Hosiery, Bridal, Accessories and a striking range of collaborations with established and up and coming designers.

The brand has a global reach, which has grown to include world-renowned stores such as Selfridges, Harvey Nichols, Luisa Via Roma and high-end luxury lingerie, fashion and concept stores world-over.

contd... Lascivious is proud to be a British brand that continues to support the UK manufacturing industry, designing & producing collections ethically in this country.

Do you have a formal lingerie design education ? I was formally trained in Contour Fashion at De Montfort University, at the time the only degree in the world specialising in lingerie.

My interest in lingerie was first piqued by a story about a friend of my mothers, who had run away to Paris to pursue her dream of becoming a lingerie designer. This glamorous tale became a driving inspiration and after completing an Art Foundation at Kingston University, my desire to move into fashion was solidified through studying different disciplines and realising that fashion would allow a cross-over of each; illustration, photography, graphic design and physical 3D design. During my period at university, I gained experience working for prestigious designers such as the late Alexander McQueen, and undertaking placements – including one at Agent Provocateur, where I was the first ever candidate to intern at the brand under the tutelage of owners Serena Rees and Joe Corre.
After graduating with a 1st Class Hons I took up a technical position with the influential Dutch modernist designer Marlies Dekkers in Rotterdam, before returning home in 2004 to found Lascivious.

What are your favourite fabrics to work with and why? I love mesh - for its stretch and versatility and its semi sheer look, stretch satin - for its luxe handle, and rigid lace - for ease of placement cutting.

What three things have inspired you lately? My inspiration is so diverse that it is difficult to pin down, I am constantly inspired by things around me - there is usually always a reference to nature, for example Ha Long bay in Vietnam was a source of inspiration for AW13, palm trees in LA for SS13. The second key component is the mood or personality of the 'muse' that I envisage for a collection, for example feminine, sporty, fierce or a combination of characters. Thirdly there would be a key shape, design line or colour that I would try to draw across the collection - for example a highlight colour or reference to a shape, such as a triangle, within the components or cut of the garments. There are always other inspirations that feed into a collection, for example recently I have been inspired by old x-rays, 60's & 70's playboy and beetles.

How do you keep your studio organised? I have an amazing team that are relatively self-regulating and cover key areas of the business. We work in an open plan studio and communicate regularly with each other. All of our computers are on a shared network, so we are able to move and share files. We also try to implement systems and guides to enable us to streamline, delegate and increase efficiency moving forward. The studio itself is split into a front showroom space and the back half is an area for sampling and technical work. The studio also has a packing area and spaces for stock. Creating specific areas, systems and regular communication allow my team to remain organised.

What motivates you? I think I have always been keen to be self-sufficient, I enjoy having control over my own situation and the direction of my career. I know that the decisions I make will affect my future, and that of my team - which sometimes can make it feel overwhelming and extremely stressful, *contd...* but is a good motivator! I'm also motivated by trying to attain a good work/life balance and the creative elements of my job.

What words of advice would you give aspiring designers? The lingerie and fashion industry is very small, don't underestimate your relationships, be discrete and professional and always strive to create something unique. There is always room for a wider selection for consumers, but with expectations and the saturation of the market increasing it is more important then ever to discover your own niche style.

Chloe Hamblen

# REVIEWS

HOW TO BECOME A LINGERIE DESIGNER

The Lingerie Journal (2012)
www.thelingeriejournal.com

> Laurie van Jonsson, accomplished intimate apparel expert, has
> written a book decoding the puzzling process for how to become
> a lingerie designer. A book addressing all aspects of becoming a
> designer, aimed at the person just starting out.

The Lingerie Lesbian (2012)
www.thelingerielesbian.com

> The balance of general overview and specific practical advice defi-
> nitely seemed to offer some clear, actionable points for if I wanted
> to become a lingerie designer. This book has a ton of information
> in it and it is well organized if you want to dip back in and reread
> a specific passage. The interviews at the end of the book with dif-
> ferent lingerie designers including Lorna Drew, Kriss Soonik,

Claire Clavering of "Kiss me Deadly" and Ayten Roberts of "Ayten Gasson". It was nice to have all these designers with diverse experiences in one place and looking at the varieties of their backgrounds.

Lingerie Talk (2012)
www.lingerietalk.com

How do you make the leap from school to launching your own lingerie brand? And is it even possible to become a designer without formal school-based training? Shockingly, there are few resources available to help aspiring designers answer those questions — until now. How To Become A Lingerie Designer is invaluable to anyone dreaming of such a career but without any concrete understanding of the business.

***** Five star review (2013)
Amazon.com

This book came right on time for me! I want to thank the author for sharing her knowledge of indie design. The fact that it focuses solely on lingerie is a big plus for me as I am working on launching a plus size lingerie line. I've searched high and low for information on the process, but like most things in the fashion arena, the things that would help a newbie are closely guarded industry secrets. I highly recommend this book, if you want to learn more about becoming an independent designer (not just lingerie either).

***** Five star review (2013)
Amazon.com

I like this book very much, because there is very much information in it of how to become a lingerie designer. She tells from her own experience and I think the book is very complete in its information. From the history of lingerie, moodboards, costings, manufacturing, photoshoots, meeting with buyers, until interviews with lingerie designers, it's all in the book. I was very happy with it!

***** Five star review (2013)
Amazon.co.uk

I teach a fashion textiles and design class and I recently discovered this book. It has become an invaluable teaching tool for my stu dents. It covers every aspect of lingerie design and offers advice and guidance in a very accessible way. I would highly recommend this book for students or people considering starting their own lingerie label or company.

Book Reviews for
The Anatomy of the Bra

Lingerie Talk (2013)
www.lingerietalk.com

Her new book, The Anatomy of a Bra, is a follow-up to last year's How To Become A Lingerie Designer, and provides a useful starting point for women who want to understand this fundamental part of their wardrobe better.

TAOAB provides a lot of technical information covering both female anatomy and the components of bra construction — all of which will be useful to design students and people working in the intimates industry. In fact, it's a sad testament to the state of the industry that most women would benefit from reading a book like this, or any of the other shelf-full of books in recent years that educate women about bra-wearing.

Handy WEBSITES

Websites to help you further your career as a Lingerie Designer.

UK MANUFACTURER
www.ajmsewing.co.uk

UK LINGERIE SAMPLE MAKING UNIT
www.lingeriesamplemaker.co.uk

HOW TO DO ALMOST ANYTHING
www.ehow.com

LIST OF LINGERIE COURSES
www.emagister.com

STYLE SITES
www.wgsn.com
www.promostyl.com

INSPIRING EZINES & MAGAZINES
www.agendamag.com
www.elle.com
www.elleuk.com
www.factio-magazine.com
www.fashioninsider.co.uk
www.fashionmagazine.com
www.fashionworlds.blogspot.com
www.flip-zone.com
www.harpersbazaar.co.uk
www.hintmag.com
www.iconique.com
www.japanesestreets.com
www.jcreport.com
www.kurvmag.com.au
www.fashioninformation.com
www.twill.info
www.vogue.co.uk

HELP WITH MOODBOARDS
www.moodshare.co
www.sampleboard.com
www.atinytribe.com
www.beeclip.com

KEEPING YOURSELF ORGANISED
www.evernote.com

SHARING IMAGES THAT INSPIRE YOU
www.pinterest.com

HELP WITH UNDERSTANDING PATTERNS
www.patternschool.com

LINGERIE/SWIMWEAR TRADE SHOWS

www.lyonmodecity.com
www.lingerie-paris.com
www.dessous.muveo.de
www.thelingeriecollective.com
www.moda-uk.co.uk
www.lingerieshow.cc/
www.swimshow.com

HELP WITH MICROSOFT EXCEL & TEMPLATES

www.office.microsoft.com

REFERENCES

Websites, Books and Images used.

Aldrich, Winifred (1985),
Metric pattern cutting, 4th ed, London: Bell and Hyman

Brockman, Helen L. (1965),
The Theory of Fashion Design, Wiley

Carter, Alison J. (1992).
Underwear: the fashion history. Batsford.

Conover, Anne (1989).
Caresse Crosby: From Black Sun to Roccasinibalda

Cox, Caroline (2000).
Lingerie: a lexicon of style. Scriptum Editions.

Ewing, Elizabeth. (1976).
Underwear: A History. New York, NY: Theatre Arts Books.

Steele, Valerie. (2001).
The Corset: A Cultural History. New Haven, CT: Yale University Press.

www.allaboutbras.co.uk/bra-guides/style-guide.php.
www.butterick.mccall.com
www.eveden.com
www.consumersearch.com/blog/breast-friends-the-bra-turns-100.
www.lingerie-uncovered.com/past/new-era.htm
www.oystermag.com/features/a-stitch-in-time.html
www.patternschool.com
www.randomhistory.com
www.researchandmarkets.com
www.simplicity.com
www.snopes.com/business/origins/bra.asp
www.voguepatterns.mccall.com

en.wikipedia.org/wiki/Brassiere
en.wikipedia.org/wiki/Caresse_Crosby
en.wikipedia.org/wiki/Lingerie
en.wikipedia.org/wiki/Market_analysis

Notes

IF YOU ANY **QUESTIONS** ON **LINGERIE** DESIGN, NEED ANY FURTHER **ADVICE** OR SIMPLY A **FREELANCER**

Please head to

www.howtobecomealingeriedesigner.com

How to become a Lingerie Designer

How to become a Lingerie Designer

Lightning Source UK Ltd.
Milton Keynes UK
UKOW04f1906260215

246989UK00001B/136/P